Understrength Air Force Officer Career Fields

A Force Management Approach

Lionel A. Galway, Richard J. Buddin, Michael R. Thirtle,
Peter S.H. Ellis, Judith D. Mele

Prepared for the United States Air Force

Approved for public release; distribution unlimited

PROJECT AIR FORCE

The research reported here was sponsored by the United States Air Force under contract F49642-01-C-0003. Further information may be obtained from the Strategic Planning Division, Directorate of Plans, Hq USAF.

Library of Congress Cataloging-in-Publication Data

Understrength Air Force officer career fields : a force management approach / Lionel A. Galway ... [et al.].
    p. cm.
  Includes bibliographical references.
  "MG-131."
  ISBN 0-8330-3699-8 (pbk. : alk. paper)
  1. United States. Air Force—Officers. 2. United States. Air Force—Occupational specialties. 3. United States. Air Force—Personnel management. 4. United States. Air Force—Job descriptions. I. Galway, Lionel A., 1950–

UG793.U52 2005
358.4'1332'0973—dc22

                                          2004023487

The RAND Corporation is a nonprofit research organization providing objective analysis and effective solutions that address the challenges facing the public and private sectors around the world. RAND's publications do not necessarily reflect the opinions of its research clients and sponsors.

RAND® is a registered trademark.

Published 2005 by the RAND Corporation
1776 Main Street, P.O. Box 2138, Santa Monica, CA 90407-2138
1200 South Hayes Street, Arlington, VA 22202-5050
201 North Craig Street, Suite 202, Pittsburgh, PA 15213-1516
RAND URL: http://www.rand.org/
To order RAND documents or to obtain additional information, contact
Distribution Services: Telephone: (310) 451-7002;
Fax: (310) 451-6915; Email: order@rand.org

Preface

In the 21st century, the technological complexity of generating and projecting aerospace power requires a myriad of different skills. Recruiting, training, and retaining people with the necessary mix of skills are major challenges for the U.S. Air Force's personnel community. Many career fields have been under strength for several years. This condition, together with the recent sharp increases in deployments (especially after the September 2001 attacks), has resulted in "stressed" career fields: too much work for too few people.

This project, conducted in RAND Project AIR FORCE's Manpower, Personnel, and Training program, examines the causes and some potential cures for understrength conditions in non-rated line officer career fields, also known as Air Force Specialties (AFSs) or, colloquially, Air Force Specialty Codes (AFSCs). Based on insights from case studies, we formulate a framework for force management that will allow understrength conditions to be diagnosed and resolved.

Understrength Air Force Officer Career Fields: A Force Management Approach describes the project, "Undermanned AFSCs," which was sponsored by the Deputy Chief of Staff for Personnel (AF/DP). It should be of value to the personnel community in the Air Force, in other services, and in the Department of Defense. Comments are welcome and should be sent to the project leader, Lionel Galway (Lionel_Galway@rand.org). Research was completed in September 2003.

RAND Project AIR FORCE

RAND Project AIR FORCE (PAF), a division of the RAND Corporation, is the U.S. Air Force's federally funded research and development center for studies and analyses. PAF provides the Air Force with independent analyses of policy alternatives affecting the development, employment, combat readiness, and support of current and future aerospace forces. Research is performed in four programs: Aerospace Force Development; Manpower, Personnel, and Training; Resource Management; and Strategy and Doctrine.

Additional information about PAF is available on our Web site at http://www.rand.org/paf.

Contents

Figures

Tables

Summary

Understrength Career Fields (see pp. 1–5)

Generating and projecting aerospace power in the 21st century are technologically complex, requiring a myriad of different skills. Recruiting, training, and retaining people with the necessary mix of skills are major challenges for the U.S. Air Force's personnel community. With the end of the Cold War, the United States armed forces began to implement a substantial reduction in total personnel, or end strength. The Air Force, for example, went from a total end strength of 571,000 in 1989 to 368,000 in 2002, despite the fact that it was involved in numerous crisis deployments, including major operations to liberate Kuwait, stop Serbian operations in Kosovo, and after 9/11, pursue parts of the war on terror in Afghanistan and Iraq. All of these events left the Air Force with severe manpower problems at the beginning of the 21st century. Many career fields were understrength: Authorizations went unfilled, and many fields had severe skill imbalances, such as a dearth of middle-level people.

This study's original charter was to examine career fields that have been "chronically and critically" under strength over time, and to look for root causes and potential solutions. We initially pursued a case-study approach, focusing on five varied career fields from the set of non-rated line officers, also known as Air Force Specialties (AFSs), or Air Force Specialty Codes (AFSCs). We found that the details of those problems and potential solutions were widely known to the managers. However, the managers had little or no access to relevant policy levers, such as accession and retention policies, which are the basic components of force management. This systemic disconnect in force management lies at the root of many of the current understrength problems. Accordingly, after consultation with our sponsor, we reoriented the project to develop an overall framework for force management that would identify roles and organizations that could provide analysis and diagnosis of understrength conditions and could also execute appropriate policy interventions to solve the problems.

The Force Management Framework (see pp. 7–14)

The Air Force needs a workforce with a balanced skill and experience mix; maintaining such a workforce that meets Department of Defense (DoD) and economic—i.e., budget—constraints requires that determination of personnel requirements, accessions, retention, education and training, assignments, and promotions be managed closely and attentively. Further, such management must be performed at three different levels (which we denote by the familiar military terms of tactical, operational, and strategic):

- Tactical: the assignments of individual officers and their individual careers.
- Operational: individual career fields (or a set of closely related fields).
- Strategic: the total Air Force workforce, including overall force size, officer/enlisted and component mix (i.e., active, Guard, Reserve, civil service, contractor), and the balance between individual career fields.

Understrength Issues for Individual Career Fields (see pp. 15–55)

The case-study career fields for our detailed analysis were electrical engineering, acquisition, personnel, communication-information systems, and intelligence. Our research (our own data analysis for the case studies, review of previous Air Force work, and discussions with managers both of the selected career fields and of the Air Force workforce as a whole) revealed chronic manning problems: For example, the Air Force has attracted enough lieutenants to meet end-strength requirements, but severe problems exist in meeting experience requirements in many occupations (e.g., in many career fields there are too few middle-level people). The problem is that most career-field management activities concentrate on decisions for *tactical* problems. These short-term problems are formidable and leave little time for managing longer-term operational and strategic issues reflecting a career field's health.

Force Management in the Air Force: Challenges, History, Current Initiatives (see pp. 57–64)

We argue that the root of understrength problems is gaps in force management, particularly at the operational and strategic levels. Operational-level force management is the key to force management as a whole. It provides both the policy framework that guides tactical-level management *and* the basic informational input for strategic-level decisions. Strategic-level management transcends operational management to allocate resources among career fields, possibly changing their structure and function.

Currently, the Air Force is oriented toward tactical activities because of the continuous near-term pressures to fill empty positions, coupled with an organizational structure that tends to emphasize a decentralized approach toward achieving objectives. The force drawdown of the 1990s has only exacerbated this phenomenon by reducing the number of people available to do force management at any level.

Conclusions and Recommendations (see pp. 65–73)

While the lack of force management does not cause all of the Air Force's understrength problems (such as competition from private-sector firms that drain away experienced people), it does inhibit diagnosis of problems and the formulation of effective responses to those problems across the service.

Doing the Operational Job

Operational-level force management, the management of career fields or career-field families, requires two distinct skill sets: substantive knowledge of the career field and knowledge of how to manage a dynamic, closed, hierarchical personnel system. The latter management skill, generic across career fields, is generally missing in operational-level management. We recommend

- making the career field manager (CFM) a full-time position (currently it is usually part-time[1]), and putting a senior functional officer in the position.
- providing the CFMs with dedicated and standardized analytic support.

Doing the Strategic Job

The strategic management job is the most difficult and important for the long-term health of the force. Essentially the locus where resources are allocated so that the Air Force has the balanced force it needs, this job sometimes requires making explicit decisions about which career fields get such resources as bonus payments, requiring making trade-offs among career fields and accepting those trade-offs. Our recommendations are to

- establish strategic-level personnel decisionmaking in a senior body with authority to make decisions for the Air Force.

----

[1] As of this writing, late 2003.

- provide the strategic-level decisionmaking body with a full-time staff, including access to analytic support that is integrated with the analytic support provided for operational management.

Doing the Tactical Job

One half of tactical-level management already has a good process in place in the Air Force: the process of assigning officers to their next job. The other half is defining longer-term career goals and plans for individual officers, which has received less consistent attention (although, with the introduction of development teams to review each officer's records regularly, it has become the focus of current changes in Air Force personnel management). We recommend that the Air Force

- provide the development teams and assignment teams with clear operational- and strategic-level guidance for managing individual careers and making assignments.

Acknowledgments

Working on a problem as broad as this required the help of many parts of the Air Force personnel community. We have attempted to make the list below as complete as possible, and we apologize in advance if we have missed anyone. The ranks, positions, and organizations of people are those as of our discussions with them during our project (mostly in FY2003).

We owe particular thanks to our action officers at the office of the Air Force Deputy Chief of Staff for Personnel (AF/DP): Mr. David Mulgrew (AF/DPLF) and Col Nancy Weaver (AF/DPLT).

At the Air Force Personnel Center (AFPC) at Randolph AFB, Texas, we thank the following: Col Michael Schiefer (DPS); Col Nellie Riley (DPAS) and her staff, particularly LtCol Tony Amadeo, Maj Thomas Layne, and LtCol Jeff Gatcomb; LtCol John Taylor and staff (DPAOO); LtCol Kenneth Gaines and Maj Robert Berger (DPASC); and last (but certainly not least), Dr. Jerry Ball and LtCol John Crown (DPSA). In addition, we had very helpful interviews with Mr. Vaughan Blackstone (DPAPP) and Mr. Dennis Miller (DPPAO). Also at Randolph, we were briefed on the responsibilities and methodologies of the Air Force Manpower & Innovation Agency (AFMIA) by LtCol Doug Carroll.

On the Air Staff, we thank Col Steve Wagoner (AF/DPXP); Col Craig Kimberlin and LtCol Mark Hays in the office of the Secretary of the Air Staff (SAF)/AQRE; LtCol Raymond Harwood, Maj Gary Leong, and Maj David Morgan in SAF/AQXD; Col John Hesterman (Air Force Senior Leader Management Office); Ms. Christal Ayo, Ms.

Genie Catchings, Maj Tony Veerkamp, Maj Steve Forsythe, and Capt Mike Anderson (Air Force Personnel Operations Agency); Maj David Cloe and LtCol Peter Read (AF/XOI); LtCol Sheron Bellizan (AF/ILCX) and LtCol John Clarke (AF/XI); and LtCol Dan Fogarty (AF/DPLFC).

We greatly appreciated advice during our research from the following RAND colleagues (in alphabetical order): Ray Conley, Gary Massey, Craig Moore, Al Robbert, and Mike Schiefer.

Finally, we appreciate the thoughtful and painstaking RAND internal technical review by Ron Sortor and Harry Thie. RAND research communicator Jennifer Li also provided valuable insights on organization. In addition, the following people sent in thoughtful comments and suggestions on the original draft: Maj Gen Peter Sutton and his staff in AF/DPL; Mr. James Barone, Air Force Materiel Command (AFMC)/DP; and LTC John Taylor at AFPC/DPAOO.

As always, any remaining errors are the sole responsibility of the authors.

Abbreviations and Acronyms

ACC	Air Combat Command
ACE	Aerospace Communications and Information Expertise
ACOT	Advanced Communications and Information Officer Training
ADSC	Active Duty Service Commitment
AEF	Air Expeditionary Force
AETC	Air Education and Training Command
AF/DP	Air Force Deputy Chief of Staff for Personnel
AF/ILC	Air Force Deputy Chief of Staff for Installations and Logistics, Directorate of Communications Operations
AF/XI	Air Force Deputy Chief of Staff for Warfighting Integration
AFAS	Air Force Assignment System
AFB	Air Force Base
AFI	Air Force Instruction
AFIT	Air Force Institute of Technology
AFMAN	Air Force Manual
AFMC	Air Force Materiel Command

AFMIA	Air Force Manpower & Innovation Agency
AFOATS	Air Force Officer and Accession Training School
AFPC	Air Force Personnel Center
AFPC/DPAS	Air Force Personnel Center/Mission Support Officer Assignments, Directorate of Assignments
AFPC/DPSA	Air Force Personnel Center/Plans, Analysis, and Information Delivery Division, Directorate of Operations
AFPOA	Air Force Personnel Operations Agency
AFS	Air Force Specialty
AFSC	Air Force Specialty Code
AFSLMO	Air Force Senior Leader Management Office
AFSPC	Air Force Space Command
AIA	Air Intelligence Agency
AIPB/PBA	aerospace intelligence preparation of the battlespace/predictive battlespace analysis
ALEET	Acquisition and Logistics Experience Exchange Tour
AMS	Assignment Management System
AO	Assignment Officer
AOC	Air Operations Center
APDC	Acquisition Professional Development Council
ASBC	Air and Space Basic Course
AV	Audio-visual
BCOT	Basic Communications and Information Officer Training
BPOC	Basic Personnel Officer Course

C4ISR	command, control, communications, and computers; intelligence, surveillance, and reconnaissance
CFM	career field manager
CGO	company-grade officer
CMDB	Consolidated Manpower Data Base
CSAF	Chief of Staff of the Air Force
CSS	Computer System Squadron
DAU	Defense Acquisition Univrsity
DAWIA	Defense Acquisition Workforce Improvement Act
DoD	Department of Defense
DOPMA	Defense Officer Personnel Management Act
DRU	Direct Reporting Unit
DT	development team
EBB	electronic bulletin board
EE	Electrical engineering
FDC	Force Development Council
FDO	Force Development Office
FDSO	Force Development Support Office
FGO	Field Grade Officer
FOA	Field Operating Agency
GO	General Officer
ISR	intelligence, surveillance, and reconnaissance
IT	Information Technology
MAJCOM	Major Command
MANPER	Manpower and Personnel
MC&G	Mapping, Charting, and Geodesy

MPF	Military Personnel Flight
NRLOAC	Non-rated Line Officer Accession Conference
OPD	officer personnel development
OPEX	Operation Experience
OTS	Officer Training School
OVAS	Officer Volunteer Assignment System
PAF	Project AIR FORCE
PEO	Program Executive Officer
PERSCO	Personnel Support for Contingency Operations
RIF	Reduction in Force
ROTC	Reserve Officer Training Corps
S&E	science and engineering
SAF	Secretary of the Air Force
SAF/AQRE	Assistant Secretary of the Air Force (Acquisition)/Science, Technology, and Engineering
SAF/AQXD	Assistant Secretary of the Air Force (Acquisition)/Acquisition Career Management and Resources Acquisition Integration
SERB	Selective Early Retirement Board
SES	Senior Executive Service
SPEED	Special Program Experience Exchange Duty
SSB	Special Separation Bonus
STP	Student, Transient, and Personnel Holdee
TAFSC	Total Active Commissioned Service
TFCFR	Total Force Career Field Review

THRMIS	Total Human Resources Management Information System
TICS	Time in Commissioned Service
TPR	Trained Personnel Requirement
USAFA	United States Air Force Academy
VSI	Variable Separation Incentive

CHAPTER ONE

Understrength Career Fields

With the end of the Cold War, symbolized by the destruction of the Berlin Wall in 1989 and the subsequent dissolution of the Soviet Union, the United States armed forces began to implement a substantial reduction in total personnel (end strength), designed to size the force for a new international security environment free of superpower conflict. The Air Force, for example, went from a total end strength of 571,000 in 1989 to 368,000 in 2002 (U.S. Census Bureau, 2004). Even the first Gulf War in 1990-1991 did not reverse the reduction in numbers, and the drawdown was completed in the first half of the 1990s. However, the Gulf War left two large deployments in place to enforce the no-fly zones imposed on Iraq at the war's end: Northern Watch and Southern Watch. Enforcing these zones required substantial Air Force resources. In addition, the Air Force was called on to undertake numerous other deployments for crises large and small, culminating in the operations against Serbia in 1999 to prevent ethnic cleansing in Kosovo; worldwide operations in response to the attacks of September 11, 2001; operations in Afghanistan against the Taliban and al-Qaeda; and the second Gulf War in 2003 to topple the regime of Saddam Hussein in Iraq.

When added to the conflicts of 1999–2003 and combined with a reduced Air Force force structure, this fast tempo of frequent and extended deployments in the 1990s (termed "boiling peace" by General John Jumper, among others) put substantial burdens on the service. Finally, an excellent economy in the 1990s, especially in the technology sector, attracted people with many of the same skills required by the Air Force.

All of these events left the Air Force with severe manpower problems at the beginning of the 21st century. First, many career fields, such as those in science and engineering, were under strength: authorized positions went unfilled. Second, many of these understrength career fields also had severe skill imbalances: a dearth of middle-level people (this was also true of some fields that were nominally fully manned—i.e., total numbers matched authorizations, but skill and experience distributions did not).[1] There was also the possibility that, for some fields, even nominally full manning might not alleviate the stress placed on them by current operational demands. For example, high-demand/low-density assets could be completely manned but in such demand that they are always deployed.

Because of these ongoing problems, especially with the prospect of increased operational tempo (optempo) as part of the operations against global terrorist organizations, the AF/DP asked RAND in 2002 to look at the problem of understrength career fields.

Evolution of Project Scope

The original charter of this study was to examine career fields—sets of Air Force officers who have similar backgrounds and responsibilities and who are managed as a group[2]—that have been "chronically

---

[1] The Air Force completed a Total Force Career Field Review (TFCFR) in summer 2001. It looked at the manning situation for each separate career field in the service, both in active forces and the reserves, and for officers and enlisted personnel. Unfortunately, the terrorist attacks in September derailed plans to follow through on the insights gained.

[2] In the personnel community, "career field" is used interchangeably with Air Force Specialty Code (AFSC; a 5-character identifier for a set of similarly skilled or trained people) and with Air Force Specialty (AFS; the first three characters of the AFSC). Air Force Instruction (AFI) 36-2101 (U.S. Air Force, 2001a) defines *career field* as "a group of closely related AFSs (or a single AFSC) when there are not related specialties) requiring basically the same knowledge and skills." In most contexts, there is no confusion. For this reason, one can refer to electrical engineers or to AFSC 62ExE (the fourth position indicates experience level and is suppressed when talking about an entire career field with all experience levels).

and critically" understrength over time, and to look for root causes and potential solutions. Because of the variety of career fields in the Air Force, our initial approach was to select several diverse fields and do case studies of those fields. Such case studies would attempt to link understrength problems in a selected field to specific issues, such as accessions and alterative civilian opportunities. In particular, we were looking for problems that would not be evident to those organizations responsible for managing individual career fields. As part of our research, we also examined previous AF work on career-field management issues, such as the Total Force Career Field Review (TFCFR), and reviewed documents such as the draft Air Force Instruction (AFI) on force development for officers (U.S. Air Force, 2001b).

As we discuss in Chapter Three, each of our selected career fields had different problems, the details of and potential solutions to which were widely known among those career field managers (CFMs). However, the CFMs had little or no access to the relevant policy levers, such as the allocation of accession targets by academic degree, bonus policy, and career path specification.. This systemic disconnect in force management lies at the root of many of the current understrength problems.

Accordingly, after consultation with our sponsor, we reoriented the project to develop an overall framework for force management that would identify roles and organizations that could provide analysis and diagnosis of understrength conditions and could also execute appropriate policy interventions to solve the problems.

At this point, we should note that managing a closed, hierarchical personnel system such as the Air Force is inherently different, and more difficult, than managing a workforce in the private sector, in which lateral entry is possible at most levels of experience. In contrast, the Air Force develops senior people in each career field, and those senior people, in turn, develop junior officers who join the service in their early or mid-20s. Managing such a force requires careful attention to accessions, retention, promotion policies, career training opportunities, and career broadening. The sequential, multiyear aspect of managing the force requires a deep understanding of the dynamics of a system in which several years of high attrition can cause deficits that persist for a decade or more. Such a system requires sophisticated analysis and modeling to understand and manage, especially in working out the effects of policy changes on the shape of the force for years to come (for example, U.S. Air Force, 1978; Walker et al., 1991; and Taylor et al., 2001).

USAF Force Management: A Moving Target

The Air Force has not stood by while optempo has increased and middle-level staff population has decreased. Over the past few years, the Air Force has been in the process of dramatically modifying its personnel management system. It has merged the manpower and personnel career fields, created the Air Force Senior Leader Management Office (AFSLMO), the Personnel Strategic Plan (U.S. Air Force, 2004), and the Chief of Staff of the Air Force's (CSAF's) sight pictures on force development (U.S. Air Force 2003b, 2003c, and 2003d).

During the year of our study, the Air Force developed several drafts of a new AFI for officer management. The AFI specified new organizations with responsibilities for managing career fields and the careers of individual officers (U.S. Air Force, 2003a). Because our findings on career-field management have direct implications for the Air Force initiatives in that AFI, we defer detailing those initiatives to the end of the report, where we make our recommendations.

However, because our case studies required us to interview the career field managers for our selected fields, we note here that one aspect of the AFI is to vest many career field management functions in a development team. A *development team* (DT) is made up of senior officers in the career field and is chaired by the career-field functional manager, usually a general officer. The development team will be responsible for monitoring the career paths of individual officers, defining potential career paths for the field, and participating in general career-field management to an extent to be determined as the new AFI is refined and implemented. For that reason, in our case studies we include some information on how the development team is being organized in each career field and what its activities are. Such information is relevant to illuminating force management issues.

Structure of the Report

Chapter Two lays out some of the dimensions of having a career field that is under strength, noting in particular that overall numbers in a field are not the only way that understrength problems arise. It then sets out the framework for force management that we developed. Chapter Three brings together the material from the case studies and explores the relationship of that material to the force management framework to show that many understrength problems result from gaps in Air Force force management, then analyzes those gaps in detail to determine what is lacking and what can be done to fill the gaps. Chapter Four summarizes how current Air Force initiatives address some of the challenges in Air Force force management. Chapter Five summarizes what this research suggests about desirable modifications to those initiatives, makes recommendations, and closes with suggestions for future research.

CHAPTER TWO

Defining Understrength Conditions and the Force Management Framework

A first task is to define what "chronically and critically understrength" means. Looking at the Air Force as a whole, one could argue that the Air Force is *not* understrength: Each year, the Air Force meets or comes close to meeting congressionally authorized end-strength levels. However, this fact raises the question of whether the personnel strength authorized by Congress is in fact consistent with the overall requirements placed on the Air Force, especially in the wake of 9/11 and the resulting increase in operations.

But even if the overall end-strength authorizations are correct and are filled in total, a given career field may not be 100-percent manned.[1] Moreover, although the overall manning levels in different career fields are certainly important, they may still mask imbalances within career fields. For example, let us consider a career field in which field-grade (majors and lieutenant colonels) and senior captain levels are manned at 75 percent and the lieutenant level is at 300 percent. Even if the career field's manning is technically at or over 100 percent, the few experienced captains and field-graders must shoulder

---

[1] For example, officers and enlisted personnel awaiting training, or in school, count against Air Force total end strength, but they are not present for duty on the active rolls of any unit. Overall, in the Student, Transient, and Personnel Holdee (STP) account, somewhere between 7 and 9 percent of total active-duty personnel is not available for unit manning. Some Air Force analysts have argued in internal papers and briefings that the STP account is responsible for much of the understrength problem. However, more analysis needs to be done. And some units are given special, 100-percent manning priority, driving the remaining units' manning even lower.

a dual burden of performing the mission, including the bulk of deployments, plus training a surfeit of lieutenants.

By how much must a career field be short-handed in order to be labeled as "critically understrength"? The answer varied widely across the various organizations in which we conducted discussions, and in no case were precise definitions known or offered. That definitions and numbers are not currently adequate to capture career-field challenges is evidenced by the somewhat subjective method by which "stressed" career fields were recently identified (i.e., functional representatives and senior leaders discussed challenges and arrived at a list largely by consensus) (Hafemeister, 2002, p. 15).

Manning issues are important—especially now. The Air Force is substantially smaller than it was just a decade ago, and deployments have increased fourfold in that same period. Therefore, any career-field shortage or grade- and skill-level imbalance within career fields is felt far more by Air Force people now than during the Cold War, when manpower was more robust and the force posture was more stable at home stations. Long-term workload surges in the aftermath of 9/11 only add to the stress on the troops. Getting Air Force requirements and manning levels right has never been more important.

Diagnosing, Understanding, and Rectifying Understrength Conditions

Early in this study, our research team was struck by the complexity of the many processes and entities involved in populating, moving, developing, and sustaining the force. In approaching an analysis of understrength career fields, it was apparent that, beyond the need to quantitatively examine issues of available "faces" against required "spaces," there was a more fundamental need to explore how the force is managed corporately, why force management is structured as it is, and whether processes, teams, and tools might be used to manage the force in a more efficient and effective manner.

First, there are scores of career fields. Each career field has unique functional requirements and challenges in terms of appropriate entry/follow-on qualifications, assignment distributions, broadening opportunities/needs/constraints, career paths/progression, civilian employment opportunities, etc. To the extent that these challenges and requirements can be independent of or even in conflict with those of other career fields, it is evident that "one-size-fits-all" force management schemes can be inherently unwieldy—or even counterproductive.

Second, myriad entities are involved in managing the force, from recruiters, commissioning sources, technical schools, and accessions personnel, to commanders, Major Command (MAJCOM) staffs, Air Force Personnel Center (AFPC) assignment teams, functional managers, manpower experts, Air Staff offices charged with generating the TPR (Trained Personnel Requirement), etc. These organizations act across all levels, from the individual airman to entire career fields to the total force: active, Guard/Reserve, civilian, and contractor. The actions of each force management entity, such as changing job requirements and setting assignment policies, affect one or more of the other entities, as well as the individuals and career fields that these actions target directly. However, our early interviews with personnel from each of these organizations highlighted that some entities and some processes are not linked. In fact, they often operate independently of each other, with autonomous policies and procedures that often are not coordinated, resulting in inefficient or counterproductive force management decisions. For example, according to interviews with senior officials in commissioning sources, accession goals for different academic degrees were based on historical accessions for different degrees instead of requirements-based targets that might be generated through linkage with the projected Air Force TPR.

Since these organizations' perceptions, policies, and actions all affect the manning of individual fields and the Air Force as a whole, it is useful to step back from the welter of force management organizations and their overlapping concerns with individual officers, specific career fields, and the total Air Force, to set up a framework for force management that will structure our study of understrength career fields.

Goal of Force Management

To carry out its missions, the Air Force needs a workforce with the "right" skill and experience mix. Several workforce dimensions are important:

- **A balanced skill mix is critical.** That is, the Air Force needs the right *mix* of skills. Numbers required in each individual skill will vary by skill and by mission. As a technology-oriented service, the Air Force must have a wide variety of skills to provide aerospace power at the right places and the right times. The mix is very broad: pilots (combat and airlift), air traffic controllers, maintenance personnel, meteorologists, munitions builders and loaders, intelligence analysts, and a variety of support service providers for the bases from which missions are flown. If certain skills are missing, or even thinly spread, overall capability can be degraded—even if other skill groups are at (or above) strength and perform at their best level.
- **The experience/grade mix must be balanced within skills.** The force must also be balanced in *experience and grade*. For example, there must be sufficient experienced intelligence officers and senior enlisted personnel to train new intelligence lieutenants. Engineers fresh out of college want experienced engineers to mentor them and help them learn the practical side of their profession.
- **The mix of active, Guard/Reserve, civilian, and contractor personnel must be determined.** Each component of the total force has unique characteristics and strengths, and the job demands of individual career fields require different mixes of each component.
- **Individual career growth must be promoted**. The active-duty Air Force has little lateral entry in most career fields, so it must develop skills from the most-junior to the most-senior levels. Development is also critical to manning the force. The Air Force relies on volunteers, so individuals must see the potential for satisfying career growth in the Air Force. Patriotism, adventure,

and energy are important motivators, but the Air Force competes for personnel with the civilian economy.

Further, the goal of a balanced force across these dimensions must be met within a set of constraints imposed on Air Force personnel policy. Budget constraints limit the total Air Force end strength, and legislation such as the Defense Officer Personnel Management Act (DOPMA) constrains the numbers in individual ranks. Other constraining policies include specifying promotion rates for certain career fields. And external conditions, such as differential civilian employment opportunities for various career fields, lead people out of the Air Force and into the private sector.

Maintaining a workforce that is balanced by skill and experience, that provides attractive career paths, and that meets Department of Defense (DoD) and economic constraints requires close and attentive management. For the purposes of this report, we define *force management* as the processes that shape and maintain the Air Force personnel structure to meet the goals of the service within the imposed constraints.

Framework for Force Management

As we define it, force management has two aspects. The first is the set of management processes that carry out personnel functions, processes that include

- Requirements determination. How many people are required for the tasks that need to be done, in peace and in war?
- Accessions. How many new personnel need to be brought in to each career field to sustain the force?
- Retention. How many people at each skill level will leave a career field? Can they be provided incentives to stay? Which fields need the incentives, and which fields will get them?

- Education and training. What set of educational opportunities are needed to give people in career fields their initial skills and what set of educational opportunities are needed to keep them up to date? Who should provide the training?
- Assignments. What sets of assignments are needed to provide people with the skills they need as they progress in a career field? How are people assigned to their next position?
- Promotions. What are the criteria for promotions? Should the criteria differ among career fields? Are all career fields treated equitably?
- Separations. How do careers end? Should there be policies, for example, to ease transition to the civil service workforce for certain career fields?

Achieving the desired force by carrying out each of these processes while satisfying the constraints requires force management at three different levels, each requiring a different scope of authority, responsibility, and information. The second aspect of force management is clearly defining and understanding the different levels; this is crucial in pinpointing where different types of problems such as understrength situations arise and how they need to be addressed.

We categorize force management in the Air Force into three levels, using the familiar military terms of strategic, operational, and tactical. These levels form the basis for the rest of our discussions on how force management affects the occurrence and solution of understrength conditions.[2]

---

[2] Current Air Force publications on leadership development use these same three terms, but in a slightly different sense. In the leadership context, *tactical, operational,* and *strategic* refer to the level of experiences and leadership competencies of individual officers. For example, tactical training is for junior officers and aims to develop competence in their career fields and effective leadership of small groups. See the website of AF/DPXF on Air Force Leadership Development, https://www.dp.hq.af.mil/dpx/dpxf/fdld/intro.htm.

Tactical

The tactical level of force management is concerned with the individual officer and his/her individual career. This level of management has two functions:

1. First and foremost, it makes assignments to fill current vacancies with qualified personnel.
2. Subject to the constraints imposed by the first function, it develops long-term career plans for individuals based on the needs of the Air Force and individual preferences. These career plans should be based in policies for the specific career field, including planning and mentoring for a career path, deciding on broadening opportunities and their timing, and counseling on education and training opportunities—among them technical education and professional military education.

Operational

The operational level of force management focuses on the individual career field (or a set of closely related fields). At this level, attention goes to maintaining overall strength in the field, developing requirements, matching the experience and grade mix with those requirements, and monitoring the career field's retention and accession numbers to sustain the career field or to overcome problems.

This level is also where career paths are defined and experience qualifications are set and validated for specific positions. In particular, this level should ensure that experience requirements and career paths are mutually feasible—i.e., that people with the needed experience can in fact be developed, given the numbers required and people available, and the training capacity and job availability.

Some career fields depend on substantial cross flows to sustain themselves—for example, the authorizations for acquisition manager officers are skewed toward senior grades, which are filled by cross flow from the scientist and engineer career fields. The operational level of management needs to set policies and coordinate with the supplying and receiving fields to ensure that both fields stay healthy.

Strategic

The strategic level of force management is concerned with overall end strength of the Air Force, and the assurance that all individual career fields are balanced in size and experience mix to accomplish the Air Force mission. In the broadest sense, linkage of Air Force personnel strategy with overall investments in people must be ensured. Ensuring this linkage includes verifying that the requirements in each career field are valid and feasible, that the active, Guard/Reserve, and civilian/contractor mix is correct, and that accession and retention resources are distributed to achieve the overall goal. It also includes monitoring the management of individual career fields. Implicit in the responsibilities at this level is the necessity of deciding how resources will be allocated across career fields, deciding what the force-mix parameters will be, and being willing to be the final arbiter for competing requirements.

CHAPTER THREE

Understrength Issues for Individual Career Fields: The Case Studies

As we noted in Chapter One, our original approach to the understrength issue was to conduct a set of case studies to examine understrength conditions and their causes in selected Air Force career fields. Our experiences with the case studies led to the development of the force management framework delineated in Chapter Two. In this chapter, we present the individual case studies, relating the problems and issues we found to the framework we developed.

Methodology

One of the reasons that this study was begun is that many different parts of the Air Force workforce are regarded as understrength: pilots, scientists and engineers, computer technicians, etc. To keep the project scope manageable, we concentrated on the active-duty, non-rated line officer force, a broad and diverse set of career fields that make up almost 50 percent of the officer corps. Part of our reason for this focus was that rated personnel (pilots, navigators, and air battle managers) have received much attention over the past few years, whereas non-rated, non-line officers (the professions of medicine, law, and the clergy) have special characteristics (lateral entry is available, and there is a narrow and well-defined civilian market). In addition, we elected to exclude general officers and focus on O-1s through O-6s, primarily because most general officers serve as very senior executives with broad responsibilities, almost always transcending individual career fields. Finally, given the choice between officers and enlisted personnel, we chose to look at officers; however, we note that the diversity of the non-rated line officers mirrors that of the enlisted force, and we expect that much of what we learn from studying problems in this segment of the officer corps will be transferable to the enlisted force in concept, if not in detail.

In studying our selected career fields, we relied on our own analysis of manpower and personnel files,[1] and the inputs of Air Force personnel analytical organizations, such as the Air Force Personnel Operations Agency (AFPOA) and the Air Force Personnel Center division for plans, analysis and information delivery in the directorate of operations(AFPC/DPSA). We also conducted interviews with personnel responsible for managing individual career fields (e.g., the career field managers), making individual assignments (the AFPC assignment teams), and for managing the more-aggregated force (AF/DP personnel). We also reviewed previous special personnel study initiatives, such as the briefings from the TFCFR mentioned earlier.

Figure 3.1 shows the broad range of the two broad groups of occupations among non-rated line officers: non-rated operations support, which comprises five career fields, and mission support, which comprises 22 career fields (individual AFSs) that are grouped into logistics, acquisition, and base support.

From these 27 career fields, we selected five that present a range of challenges and problems for the Air Force. We examine problems in manning these career fields over the past several years: being

---

[1] All of the analyses in this report were drawn from two data sources. The first is the Consolidated Manpower Data Base (CMDB), which is the collection of Unit Manpower Documents from each unit in the Air Force. This database provides the count of authorized positions for each career field and is managed by the Division of Data Systems, Directorate of Manpower and Organization, Air Force Deputy Chief of Staff, Personnel (AF/DPMI). The other data source is the Uniform Officer Records, which contains the current job and other demographic information about each individual officer. It is maintained by the Air Force Personnel Center at Randolph AFB, Texas. Our final analyses used the versions of these databases as of September 2003, except where indicated otherwise.

Figure 3.1
Non-Rated Operations and Mission Support Career Fields

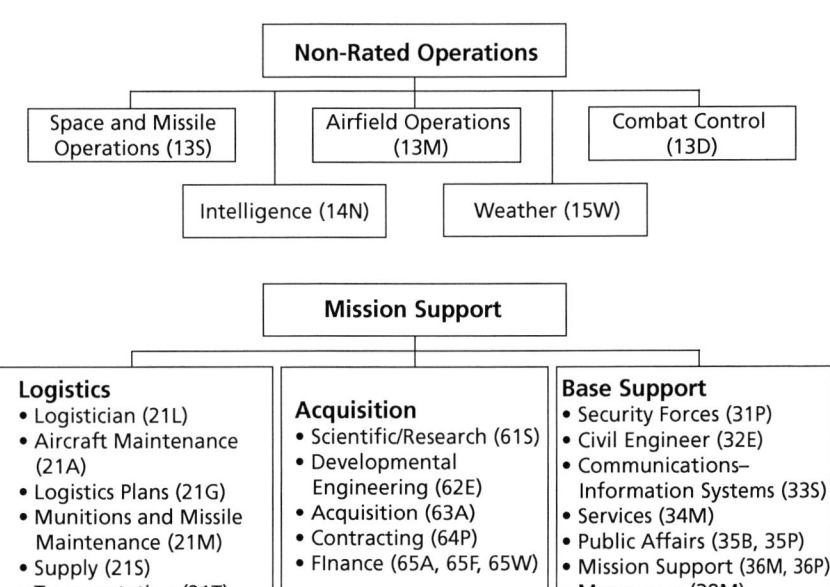

RAND *MG131-3.1*

under strength, grade imbalances, and issues in developing officer skills and experiences that are important in sustaining the career fields. After an initial review of manning problems, we examined in greater detail Intelligence, Communications–Information Systems, Personnel, Electrical Engineering, and Acquisition (AFSs/AFSCs 14N, 33S, 36P, 62ExE, and 63A, respectively) for our detailed analyses.

The remainder of this chapter is divided as follows. The next section provides an overview of the key characteristics of officers entering different occupations. We look at entry-level second lieutenants who were commissioned in the Air Force from 1999 through 2002, comparing the sources of commission, college majors, initial assignments, and prior-service content of our selected career fields with one another as well as with other non-rated line officers. With little lateral entry, the shape of career fields is largely determined by the composition of new accessions.

Following the overview of accessions, the next five sections detail specific problems in manning particular career fields. Each section is a case study of the issues facing the career field, current manning problems, and potential solutions to those problems, and uses our force management framework to structure the discussion. A final section summarizes manning problems across the career fields and considers systemic issues in addressing those problems, again in the context of the force structure framework.

One note: Our analysis here assumes that authorizations (that is, requirements) are correct; it considers career fields to be under strength if they do not meet the authorization levels. Many criticisms have been made of the process by which authorizations are determined (see, for example, Dahlman et al., 2002), some of which we will deal with in passing. The Air Force manpower community has recently "balanced the books" on authorizations,[2] and our numbers here reflect the resulting data. But there is more to be done. This question is a crucial one, for without valid targets for positions to be filled, it is hard to make any progress on determining where personnel shortages are and what to do about them. However, in this project we could not explore this important area.

Overview of New Officer Assignments

Air Force line officers are commissioned from the U.S. Air Force Academy (USAFA), the Reserve Officer Training Corps (ROTC), and Officer Training School (OTS). Each group has unique features that shape the manning profile of young officers. USAFA graduates undergo a stiff selection competition to enter the academy and are given considerable leeway in choosing their career fields. ROTC graduates enter the Air Force through two- and four-year programs and face strong incentives to undertake specific majors that the Air Force selects. OTS graduates, many of which have prior military ex-

---

[2] The "balance-the-books" initiative was an effort led by the AF/DP staff to refine, or scrub, authorizations. This effort was largely complete by June 2003.

perience in the enlisted Air Force, are selected according to the skills they have that fill short-term shortfalls in the Air Force. Many OTS officers reach retirement eligibility while still in the mid-level officer ranks.

Figure 3.2 shows that, overall, 14 percent of newly commissioned officers were from USAFA and another 35 percent were from OTS. The remaining 51 percent were drawn from ROTC programs (about 75 percent of ROTC graduates participated in the full four-year scholarship program). Note that proportions of the sources of commission for the case-study occupations differ substantially from one another and from the overall average. The communications

Figure 3.2
Commissioning Sources for Non-Rated Line Officers

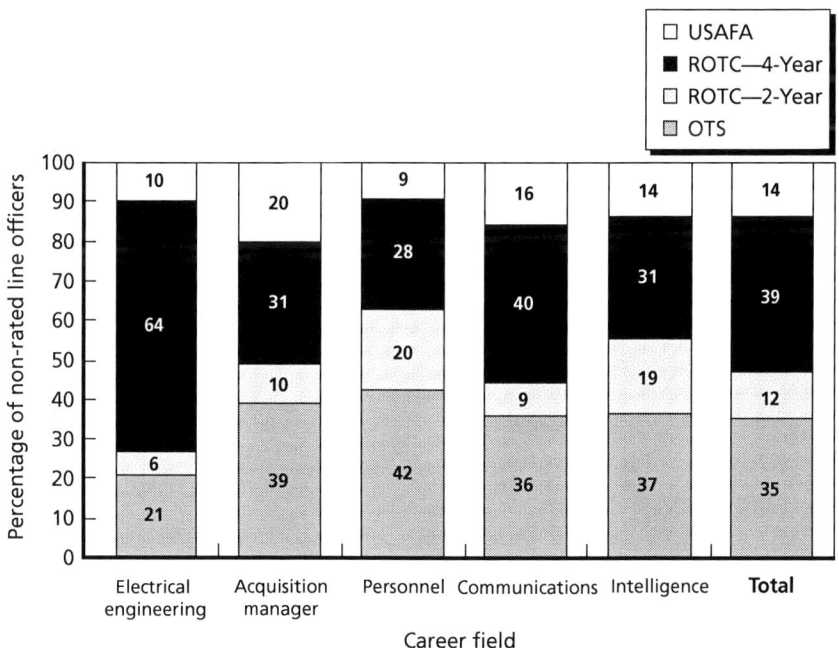

and acquisition AFSs attract larger shares of USAFA graduates, whereas fewer academy graduates enter personnel or electrical engineering.

The electrical engineering field draws officers from very different sources than the other non-rated line career fields. About 70 percent of new accessions enter the electrical engineering field from ROTC, and over 90 percent of these accessions are drawn from the four-year scholarship program. This pattern reflects that electrical engineering officers are required to have engineering degrees, whereas relatively few USAFA graduates are electrical engineers, and some of those become pilots.

Table 3.1 shows that all electrical engineer accessions (62ExE) are engineering majors. About 95 percent have electrical engineering majors (the labeling of majors is somewhat imprecise, so many of the remaining 5 percent may have skills similar to those of an electrical engineer, but have degrees in computer engineering or other disciplines). Engineers comprise about 13 and 15 percent of new accessions in communications (33S) and acquisition (63A), respectively, but few engineers enter intelligence (14N) or personnel (36P).

Unlike electrical engineers, the other selected occupations draw officers from a wide range of college majors. Liberal arts majors (social sciences; arts, humanities, and education; and administration, management, and military science) fill over 75 percent of the positions in intelligence and personnel. About 46 percent of accessions in communications are drawn from inter-area majors. Other communications accessions are broadly spread across the other majors. About 48 percent of acquisition accessions majored in administration, management, and military science, and the career field also has substantial numbers of officers with undergraduate degrees in engineering, math, and social sciences.

Table 3.1
Percentage of College Majors Among Recent Officer Accessions, by AFSC

College Major	14N	33S	36P	62ExE	63A	Total
Inter-Area (Computer Science, Operations Research)	12	46	4	0	5	12
Administration, Management, and Military Science	8	14	9	0	48	17
Arts, Humanities, & Education	18	6	29	0	3	11
Biology & Agricultural Science	2	5	10	0	2	4
Engineering	4	13	1	100	15	23
Law	1	1	1	0	1	1
Math	1	3	0	0	9	3
Medical	0	1	4	0	1	1
Physical Science	3	3	1	0	8	5
Social Science	50	9	39	0	9	22

Many newly commissioned officers are assigned to formal training before their initial duty assignments. Figure 3.3 shows that about 15 percent of second lieutenants are in STP and not yet in their first duty (permanent-party) assignment.

The STP rate for new intelligence officers is much higher than in other career fields. These officers are initially assigned to Goodfellow AFB for training, and their lengthy training is sometimes delayed by waiting for security clearances. The STP rate is also above average for engineers. STP rates are below the overall average in communications, personnel, and acquisition, which may reflect short initial training in the career field or a reluctance of career field managers to allow supplementary schooling for new entrants.

Table 3.2 shows the first permanent-party assignments of second lieutenants (many are assigned initially to STP).

Lieutenants in intelligence, communications, and personnel are concentrated in Air Combat Command (ACC) and AETC. About 82 percent of newly assigned acquisition officers are assigned to Air Force Materiel Command (AFMC). Assignments are also concentrated for electrical engineers, where 56 percent are in AFMC and another 23 percent are in the Air Intelligence Agency (AIA). About 15 percent of early intelligence assignments are in AIA.[3]

---

[3] The distribution of assignments across O-2 (first lieutenant) through O-6 (colonel) paygrades is considerably more dispersed than that for second lieutenants.

Figure 3.3
STP Rates for Second Lieutenants, by Career Field

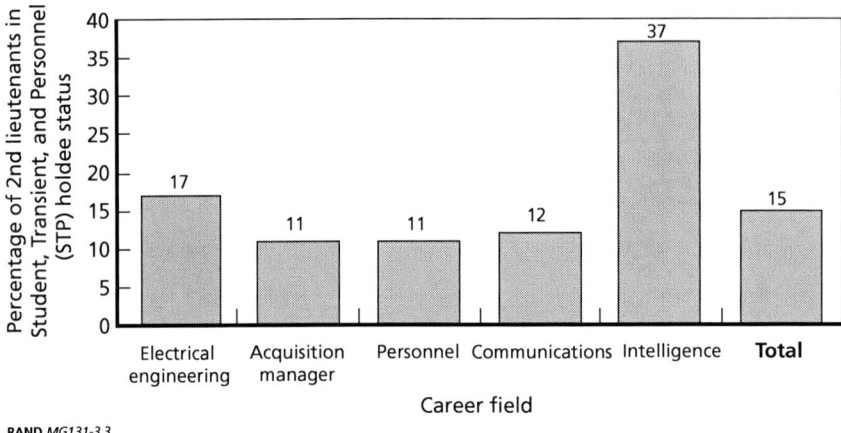

RAND *MG131-3.3*

Figure 3.4 shows that nearly a third of new non-rated line officers have prior service experience before commissioning, ranging in
our sample occupations from a high of 39 percent for communications to a low of 19 percent for electrical engineers. Prior-service officers have several years of military experience before commissioning.
Several CFMs we interviewed have said that this fact causes problems
in filling senior field-grade positions, because many prior-service offi-

Table 3.2
Percentage of Second Lieutenants Only Assigned to Key MAJCOM/Agencies,
by AFSC

MAJCOM/Agency	14N	33S	36P	62ExE	63A	Total
Air Combat	31	34	37	14	3	26
Air Education and Training	15	11	24	1	1	11
Air Mobility	8	13	12	0	2	12
Air Force Materiel	2	9	10	56	82	22
Air Force Space	2	7	7	6	9	12
Air Intelligence Agency	15	3	3	23	1	3
Air Forces in Europe	7	9	1	0	0	3
Pacific Air Forces	12	9	3	0	0	4
Other	8	6	4	1	1	6

Figure 3.4
Prior-Service Content of Recent Second Lieutenants, by Career Field

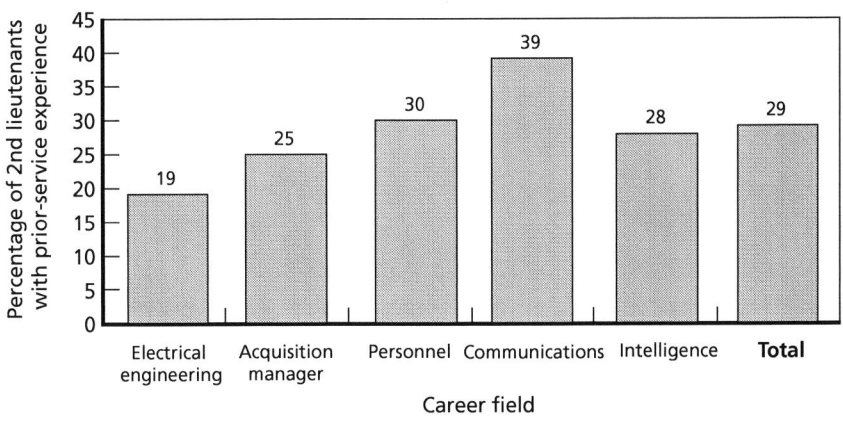

cers become eligible for retirement in captain and major ranks and leave the Air Force at that time.

A final issue of key importance is the flow of engineering graduates into the Air Force. Engineers are considered critical for performing many technical jobs in the Air Force, and several career fields require officers with engineering degrees. With little lateral entry into the Air Force and very limited cross-training of other officers into engineering billets, the supply of officers available for these engineering jobs is limited by the Air Force's ability to recruit and retain young engineers.

Figure 3.5 shows that engineers as a whole constituted 21 to 25 percent of new officers between FY1994 and FY1999. The percentage of engineers fell from 25 percent in 1999 to only 16 percent in 2002. Similarly, the percentage of officers with electrical engineering degrees declined in recent cohorts. While about 6 percent of accessions had electrical engineering degrees between 1994 and 1999, the percentage fell to only 3 percent by 2002.

Figure 3.5
Engineering Degrees for Officer Commissioning Classes of FY1994
Through FY2002

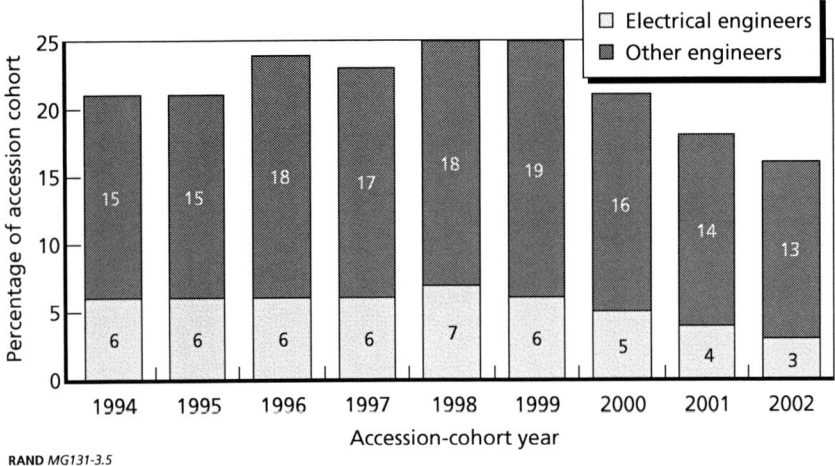

RAND *MG131-3.5*

We now turn to a more detailed examination of understrength issues in each of the five selected career fields.

Electrical Engineers

Electrical engineering (EE; AFSC 62ExE) is part of the set of engineering career fields (aeronautical, astronautical, computer, electrical/electronic, flight test, project, and mechanical). As with the other engineering fields, most electrical engineering positions are located in Air Force Materiel Command (AFMC), and a substantial number are also in direct engineering activities at laboratories and test facilities.[4] Other areas of concentration are the Air Intelligence Agency, the Air Force Operational Test and Evaluation Center, and

---

[4] Some Air Force officers with degrees in engineering are not in the engineering career field. For example, some electrical engineers are employed in the communications field; some engineers are rated officers (mainly pilots or navigators); and others are also outside the engineering and acquisition fields because of personal preference.

MAJCOM staffs, especially at ACC. EE authorizations and assignments are concentrated in the company grades (O-1 to O-3) and lower field grades (O-4), primarily because recently graduated engineers are more current than more senior officers in technical knowledge. Unless they are continually involved in engineering work and professional education, that currency can erode rapidly. As with the private sector, much of the requirement for more-senior engineering officers is in a small number of managerial positions, and there is a corresponding limitation of promotion opportunities for junior officers within the career field. Consequently, many electrical engineers, if they do not leave the Air Force, move to the acquisition career field.

The acquisition career field has proportionally fewer junior slots and depends on inflow (i.e., immigration) from engineering and scientific career fields to help fill senior positions. Other than moves to acquisition, there is little movement out of the EE career field to other areas. And, because of its technical nature, the field attracts very little immigration and little or no substitution between engineering specialties.[5]

Understrength Problems

Electrical engineering has severe understrength problems, as do several of the other science and engineering (S&E) fields. The EE field is cited the most often as chronically and critically under strength by the Air Staff and AFMC both because it is a large field and because the number of empty slots is so large: In June 2003, there were authorizations for 911 EEs of all grades, but only 679 of them were filled. Recent reviews of authorizations have reduced authorizations in some fields significantly, but substantial numbers of vacancies persist in EE: Only 75 percent of required positions are filled, and only 66 percent of those positions go beyond the lieutenant grade. Figure 3.6

---

[5] Some of the people we interviewed who manage S&E staff for the Air Force indicated that the AFSC structure may be too broad: Even within an AFSC such as 62ExE, certain subdivisions, such as microwaves and computer engineering, are difficult to cross-train in/cross over to.

shows that only 59 percent of captain positions are filled. Many Air Force career fields have met their overall end-strength requirements by having excess lieutenants, but the Air Force has only been able to recruit enough EE lieutenants to just meet its requirement for these junior officers.

Given the shortages of electrical engineers, it is at first glance surprising that so many EEs are assigned outside their career fields, particularly at the captain and major level. Figure 3.6 shows that the shortfall for captains could be reduced by 40 percent, if O-3 EEs

Figure 3.6
Assignment Patterns in Electrical Engineering

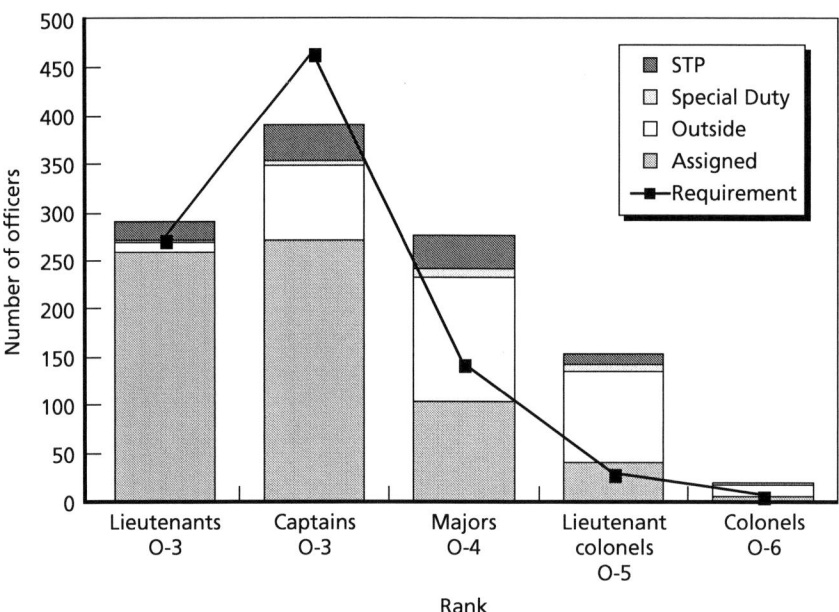

NOTE: This figure (and the analogous figures presented below for the other selected AFSCs) shows the situation as of the third quarter of FY2003. The connected set of square markers shows the requirements for EEs by grade, as reflected in Air Force manpower authorizations. The gray "Assigned" portion of each bar is the number of all officers of any AFSC who occupied a position that required an electical engineer. If the career field was perfectly manned, each grade's gray bar would meet the corresponding square. The "Outside" portion shows the number of officers with a primary or secondary AFSC in electrical engineering who are in non–electrical engineering positions, excluding special duty (duty AFSCs coded 8xxxx or 9xxxx) and the STP account. The other two portions of each bar indicate special-duty positions and those officers in the STP account.

assigned outside the career field were assigned to positions that require electrical engineers. At the ranks of major and lieutenant colonel, more EEs are assigned outside rather than inside the career field.

The substantial number of outside assignments for electrical engineers suggests that the Air Force either explicitly or implicitly is giving greater priority to these outside vacancies than to the requirement for electrical engineers. However, interviews with CFMs and assignment-team personnel indicate that they feel that important jobs are going unfilled. Yet there does not appear to be an organization that can address these trade-offs explicitly.

Figure 3.7 shows that the understrength problems in electrical engineering have grown substantially over the past decade. In 1994 and 1996, the Air Force filled 97 and 89 percent of the overall requirement for this field. Since 1996, the overall fill rate has been

Figure 3.7
Percentage of Manned Electrical Engineer Duty Assignments,
by Fiscal Year (excludes STP assignments)

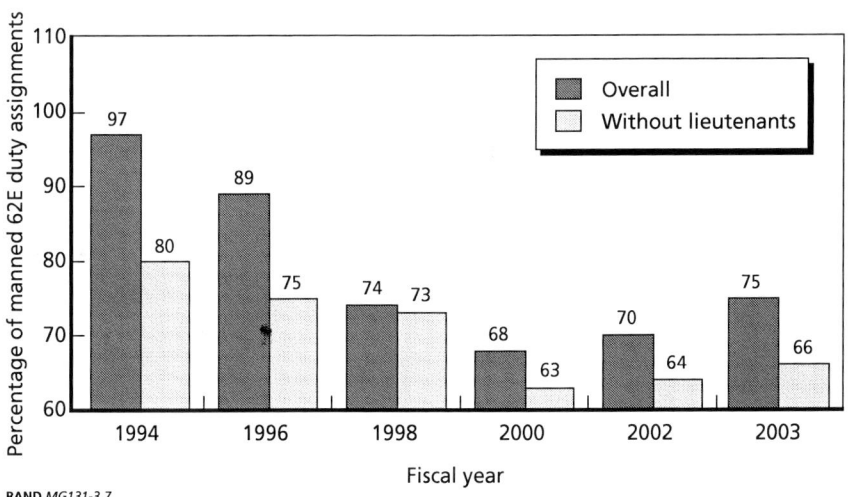

only about 72 percent. The manning picture deteriorates further if we look beyond the entry-level lieutenants. In the past several years, less than two-thirds of the captain and field-grade positions have been filled.

Much of the manning problem for the EE career field in the lower grades is attributable to a lack of linkage with accessions sources, and particularly with ROTC. Until recently, ROTC goals for engineer recruiting did not correspond directly to vacancies or projected requirements.[6] Admittedly, managing this linkage can be complex: Accession requirements are set by projecting inventories and retention rates over multiple years of service, then these numbers must drive the recruitment of freshman and sophomore engineering students—i.e., students three to four years away from commissioning.

The other major problem with this career field is retention. S&E officers in general have the highest loss rate among non-rated officers (Figure 3.8). Many young officers leave shortly after their initial obligation ends—an exodus that is attributed to the demand from the civilian sector. However, the civilian sector aside, it has also been argued that the career path for S&E officers is generally not attractive. Unfortunately, most of the information on the latter issue is anecdotal.[7]

---

[6] There are some differences of opinion about the linkage. One of the purposes of the Non-rated Line Officer Accession Conference (NRLOAC), is to help link accessions to requirements by bringing together representatives of the accession sources and the career field managers. However, we learned that some CFMs did not attend. Further, until three years ago, the S&E fields had no CFM (see later in this section). And we were told in one interview with a senior AFOATS (Air Force Officer Accessions and Training Schools, in charge of ROTC and OTS) officer that ROTC scholarships were largely apportioned among majors based on previous years' allocations.

[7] For example, one contention is that young people joining the Air Force require (and want) an experience with the flying Air Force, and so it was encouraged in the 1990s to assign a new S&E officer to an operational tour, not to an S&E position. Others argued that S&E officers are at their peak in subject-area currency when they graduate, and not using them in S&E positions wastes the Air Force's investment in their education, as well as disappointing them by separating them from the S&E world for two years. This operational-versus-S&E dilemma raises the question of whether Air Force engineers should be active-duty officers or civilians, reservists, or contractors should fill the S&E slots.

Figure 3.8
Loss Rates for Officers, by AFSC

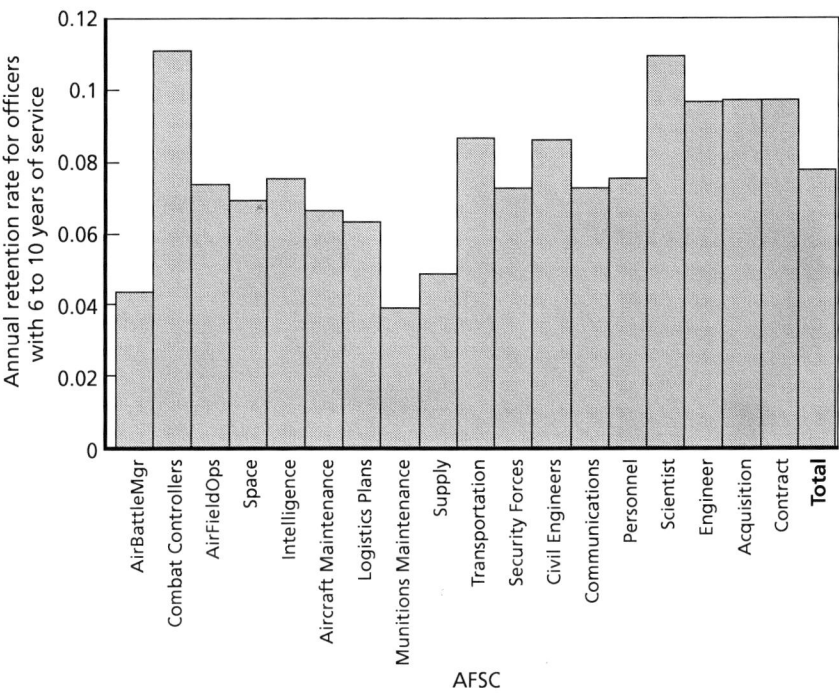

RAND *MG131-3.8*

A recent re-recruiting effort threw an extra twist into this discussion by finding that S&E officers felt isolated when assigned to organizations that were staffed primarily by civilians, and they were sometimes at a disadvantage for receiving continuing education because supervisors allocated training resources to the "permanent" staff. As noted above, technical currency erodes quickly without continuing education, and balancing this need with military requirements for career-broadening (serving outside one's career field to get broader experience in the Air Force) and staff assignments is a challenge for military engineers' careers that needs to be sorted out at the career-field level by a management structure that has the analytic resources to diagnose these competing requirements/needs and the authority and resources to resolve them.

Career-field management for EEs and for *all* USAF scientists and engineers (military and civilian) resides in the office of the Secretary of the Air Force (SAF)/AQRE (the Science and Engineering Management Division of AQR). This office dates from early 2001: unlike virtually all other AF officer career fields, and in spite of the ongoing difficulties in manning and retention, for much of the 1990s, all the S&E career fields had no CFM. During this period, these career fields experienced strong competition from the civilian economy, and had the career-path problems noted above that led to first-term retention problems. The new office has taken a fresh look at the S&E career fields, including conducting a futures study, a requirements study, a review of S&E management, and a re-recruiting effort by senior S&E officers to reach S&E officers who were nearing career decision points.

At present, the S&E community has not availed itself of outside analytic help, partly because its focus has been directed to rethinking the requirement for S&E officers rather than details of grade and experience structure, and partly because the personnel who staff the office are themselves analysts.

The AFPC assignment team for S&E officers is the Mission Support Officer Assignments, Directorate of Assignments (AFPC/DPAS). Up to the date when it was agreed that SAF/AQ would take responsibility for CFM functions for these fields, this assignment team in effect did both jobs: assignments and career-field policy. As might be expected, much of this policy focused on tactical issues, because those issues most concerned the assignment teams and because they had the most insight into and control over assignments. This policy included a decision not to release company-grade officers (CGOs) from any engineering fields except to attend the Air Force Institute of Technology (AFIT) or have an operational tour; in particular, they were not released to acquisition slots. However, a fair number of CGOs with engineering primary or secondary AFSCs are still in acquisition positions, so this policy may sometimes be overcome by other factors. Beyond decisions like this, the assignment teams can do little to affect the career field. There was limited interaction with AFOATS to try to ensure that ROTC recruiting focused on the proper majors.

That the key career-path flow is out of engineering (and the scientific AFS) into the acquisition field is recognized as an important issue and is being monitored. The CFM notes that both career fields are within the acquisition "family" of career fields,[8] and so issues arising from this flow can be handled between AQRE and AQXD (who manages the acquisition career field), or by the acquisition super-council, which has been formed from the Acquisition Professional Development Council (APDC), a body that ensured that acquisition officers and personnel had the professional training required by DoD regulations. As planned, the super-council will coordinate career-field management across the acquisition fields.[9]

Force Management Perspective

Electrical engineering clearly has a major problem with filling the sheer numbers of requirements, especially at the lower grades, where most of the requirements are. The lack of lieutenants (especially at a time when many other career fields are overstocked) indicates an accession problem, which has been attributed to the lack of linkage between actual requirements and recruiting goals. The lack of captains is due to retention problems, which may be caused by the boom economy of the late 1990s, career-path issues, or lack of accessions in the mid-1990s, or all of these. The economy slowed during 2000–2003, and opportunities for engineers may be down temporarily, helping this career field in the short run.

Numerically, requirements for majors could be filled, although with the numbers getting smaller there may be technical requirements for specific positions that the available people may not actually

---

[8] The family comprises scientists, engineers, acquisition managers, contracting, and finance.

[9] The APDC comprises key Air Force leaders (Senior Executive Service [SES] and General Officer [GO] levels) within the acquisition community: representatives from SAF/AQ (including the SAF/AQX), two-letter functionals at the Air Staff, MAJCOM Vice Commanders, Program Executive Officers (PEOs), and the DP Staff.

match, and/or the other positions in which these people are placed may be more important to fill.

It is clear that for several years real operational (in the sense of our force management framework) management of this and other S&E career fields has been lacking—a surprising finding, given the Air Force's dependence on technology. Operational management encompasses the links to accessions, earlier arguments for action on retention, and a systematic approach to career field assessment. The current CFM office is addressing these issues, but considerable remedial work must be done quickly if the career field is to recover. However, plans for analytic support and whether a balance can be achieved between career-field focus and individual career development are still unclear, awaiting the release of the AFI on force development to guide more detailed planning.

The longer-term, total-force issue of whether the Air Force needs as many officer-engineers both for filling actual engineering positions and for giving future managers vital technical experience needs to be addressed at the strategic level, balancing the needs of all the S&E career fields against the Air Force's active/reserve/civilian/contractor structure.

Acquisition Manager

The acquisition manager career field (63A; also referred to as the "program manager" career field) is one of the five acquisition AFSs,[10] which form the Air Force Acquisition Corps of officers under the Defense Acquisition Workforce Improvement Act (DAWIA).[11]

---

[10] Air Force Supplement 1 to DoDI 5000.2, *Defense Acquisition Management Policies and Procedures,* provides basic and detailed guidance for acquisition programs and use of acquisition AFSCs.

[11] This 1990 legislation specifies minimum qualification standards for those performing functions integral to the acquisition process, and it defines critical acquisition positions. The law requires DoD to develop a skilled, professional workforce by formalizing career paths for personnel who wish to pursue careers in acquisition. This formalized path includes a

Acquisition managers are responsible for the management of Air Force acquisition programs, and they advise commanders and staff on the status and progress of acquisition programs.

The typical acquisition management officer is responsible for, among other tasks, integrating engineering, program control, test and deployment, configuration management, production and manufacturing, quality assurance, and logistics support. Individual responsibilities will usually include planning, organizing, and developing program management techniques and determining organizational structure, personnel, training needs, and security requirements. Ensuring that an acquisition program is meeting cost, schedule, and performance objectives is key to success in this career field.[12] For entry into this field, an officer must have an undergraduate degree in a quantitative major (e.g., engineering, analytical/physical science, or management) or 24 hours in such areas. An officer reaches the qualified level by completing the Defense Acquisition University (DAU) acquisition coursework plus 18 months of service.

Within the acquisition corps, the acquisition manager career field provides relatively more leadership opportunities than does either the scientist or engineering field. Scientist and engineering are the fields providing the experiences that lead to promotion. Acquisition management positions are found at the Pentagon, such MAJCOMs as AFMC and the Air Force Space Command (AFSPC), and other key acquisition programs (Ballistic Missile Defense, the Joint Staff, and joint organizations). Acquisition management officers are encouraged to cross-flow into an operations-oriented career field for a limited period of time to gain a fuller understanding of how the Air Force works. An example of such a cross-flow is the Acquisition and Logistics Experience Exchange Tour (ALEET), in which highly capable acquisition officers are assigned to operational squadrons as logistics officers.

---

certification process, and specific education, training, and experience requirements for those in acquisition positions.

[12] Air Force Manual (AFMAN) 36-2105, 2001, p. 238.

Such flows of acquisition management officers out of the career field are generally expected to occur early in the officer's career, involve an experience in an operational unit, and be temporary. The same cannot be said for many scientist and engineer officers who shift to acquisition management, where they are likely to stay for the greater promotion and leadership opportunities.

Understrength Problems

Figure 3.9 provides a current snapshot of assignment patterns in acquisition management. The career field has about three times more

Figure 3.9
Assignment Patterns in Acquisition Management

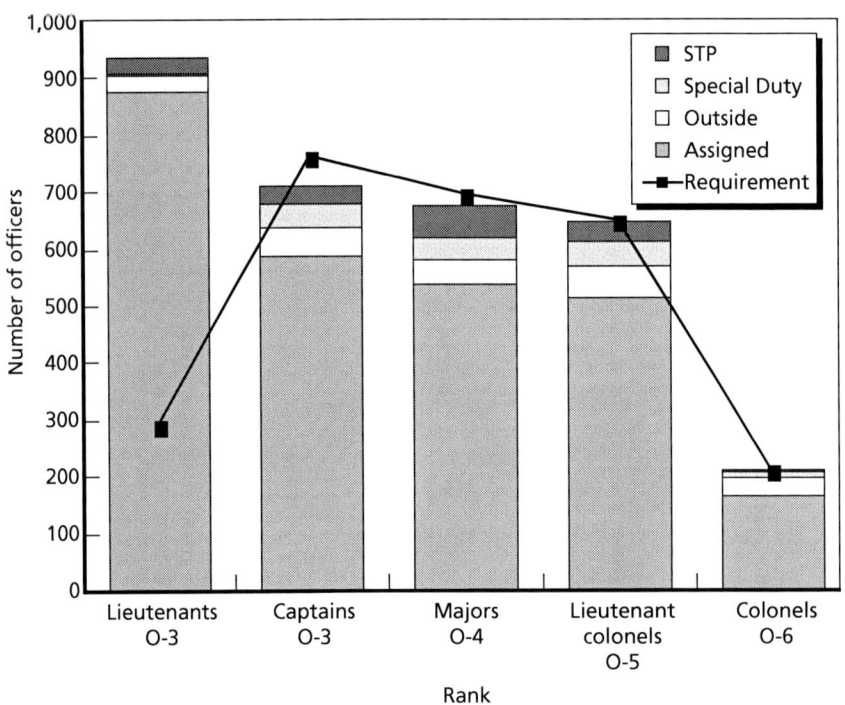

lieutenants assigned to it than it requires. But the field is consistently undermanned at higher ranks. At captain, major, and lieutenant colonel ranks, only about 78 percent of the positions are filled. The manning shortfalls could be largely offset if more acquisition officers continued in acquisition assignments. At the O-3 to O-6 grades, about 25 percent of acquisition officers are in positions that do not require acquisition officers.

Figure 3.10 shows that the Air Force has succeeded consistently in meeting overall manning levels for acquisition managers. Therefore, this is nominally a healthy career field, because it meets the Air Force criterion of a 90-percent fill rate. Yet, this success reflects largely an excess of lieutenants,[13] and the manning picture is

Figure 3.10
Percentage of Manned Acquisition Management Duty Assignments,
by Fiscal Year (excludes STP assignments)

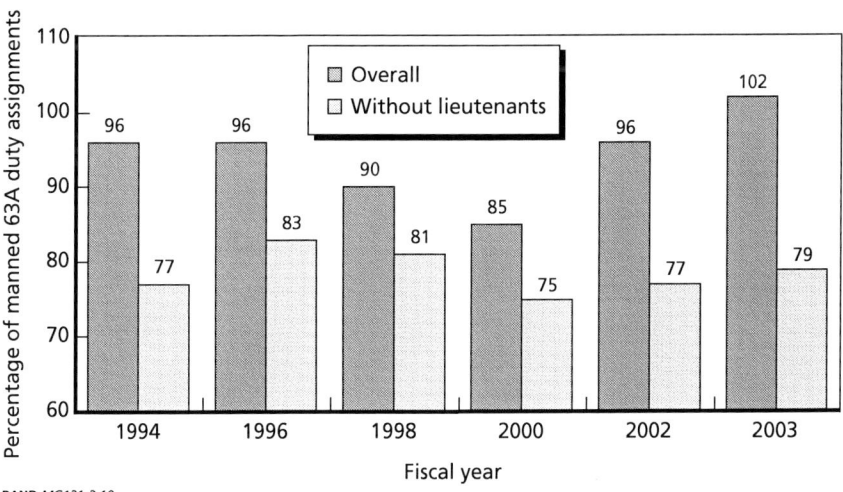

RAND *MG131-3.10*

---

[13] The exact disposition of lieutenants is unclear. Some lieutenants are assigned to slots designated for the rank of captain, particularly those for junior captains. Some lieutenant positions are multiply filled—i.e., several lieutenants are assigned to one lieutenant slot.

much weaker for captains and field-grade officers. In recent years, the Air Force has filled only 75 to 80 percent of authorizations beyond the lieutenant level.

Although retention problems in acquisition management have not been as severe as those in science and engineering, the Air Force included this field with those and several others in a retention bonus program as an incentive to stay in the Air Force.[14] As part of our study of this field, we tried to determine the analytic basis for determining the bonus payments and target personnel. However, we could find no rigorous cost-benefit analysis or econometric impact analysis that was used to determine an optimal bonus amount or target population prior to bonus implementation.[15] The success of this program has not yet been determined empirically.

SAF/AQXD is the career field manager for all acquisition management officers. DAWIA-oriented activities and a strong linkage between the responsible AFPC assignment teams and AQXD appear to have created well-worn paths that are understood by all officers in this field. We did note that the career-field management did not regularly utilize analytic organizations such as AFPOA for quantitative analysis to support CFM activities.

Force Management Perspective

From the tactical perspective, this career field is in good shape: Career paths are well defined, well understood, and well monitored. However, because having technically qualified acquisition managers depends on inflow from scientist and engineer career fields, attention must be paid at the operational and strategic levels to ensuring that

---

[14] Called the "Critical Skills Retention Bonus," the program is currently focused on five career fields: civil engineering (32E), communications and information (33S), scientific (61S), engineering (62E), and acquisition management (63A). The bonus targets officers with 4–13 years of Total Active Commissioned Service (TAFSC) and pays $10,000 per year for four years if the officer is eligible for the entire period.

[15] Obviously, bonuses plausibly provide an incentive for any career field. However, bonuses should be computed by econometric analysis of other career options. See, e.g., Gotz and McCall, 1979, and Fernandez, 1989. When resources are especially limited, bonuses need to be carefully targeted to career fields in which they will be cost-effective.

there is an adequate supply of these types of officers to man both their own career fields and acquisition management. In examining the senior company and field grades, we found that program managers have understrength issues, but the future of the acquisition management career field is not as bleak as others studied in this report. Unlike the EE field, which has a supply-shortage problem, acquisition management currently has a relative overabundance of new officers.

Besides "normal" retention challenges, such as the potential employment in the private sector of experienced project managers during good economic times, the perception of the career field is fairly bright: Project managers tend to be promoted faster than their counterparts within the Acquisition Corps, and the number of leadership opportunities is greater (as a proportion of the total personnel in the field) than for the scientists or engineers. The use of a bonus during 2003 will probably aid in offsetting any near-term losses in the senior company and field grades.

Personnel

As a result of occupational realignments in the 1990s, the personnel career field (36P) now combines personnel officers (who administered military personnel processes), those who were squadron section commanders, specialists in education and training, and equal opportunity officers. Officers in the new personnel career field are now expected to gain experience in each of these areas during their careers.

Newly commissioned personnel officers generally go to the Basic Personnel Officer Course (BPOC) at some point during their first six months of service. Personnel officers also usually receive specialized training in wartime missions through the one-week Personnel Support for Contingency Operations (PERSCO) course or the MANPER-B (Manpower and Personnel B) course. These modest training requirements mean that second lieutenants are quickly dispatched to their first assignments.

The initial three to five years in the Air Force usually are spent in base-level jobs. About two-thirds of lieutenant positions in personnel are as squadron section commanders, positions that are spread broadly across operations and support sides of the flight line, so that officers gain a broad knowledge of Air Force management skills. The other third of lieutenants are assigned as section chiefs in the base Military Personnel Flight or as education and training chiefs. After a two-year stint in one of these two types of jobs, officers are encouraged to switch to a job of the other type in order to obtain a broader range of personnel experience. A key dimension of this early experience is learning the tasks necessary for supporting expeditionary deployment organizations and units.

Understrength Problems

Overall, the personnel field is overstrength, due to a huge influx of lieutenants. Figure 3.11 shows unfilled positions in the O-3 through O-6 grades.

Personnel officers are encouraged to broaden their knowledge of the Air Force by taking assignments outside the career field, in outside or special-duty assignments. The shortfalls in the captain and field grades could readily be met if more personnel officers remained in 36P assignments. The most common nonpersonnel assignments for captains and majors are as instructors, as executive officers, in operations support, and in communications-information systems. Only 78 percent of personnel officers who are not in STP status are actually in 36P assignments. (Officers from other core[16] AFSCs fill some personnel assignments.) On net, however, the personnel career

---

[16] "Core" has a specialized meaning in the Air Force personnel community. For non-rated officers, "core" career field is indicated by their primary AFSC, which forms the basis for their assignments and management. Officers can get secondary AFSCs, indicating other competencies, but shifting "out of core" takes official approval from both the losing and gaining career fields. However, officers can be assigned "out of core" for career broadening or because of understrength conditions, although they usually return to their core field in either case. In some specialized career fields, such as engineering, it is rare to have assignments from out of core into the field.

Figure 3.11
Assignment Patterns in Personnel

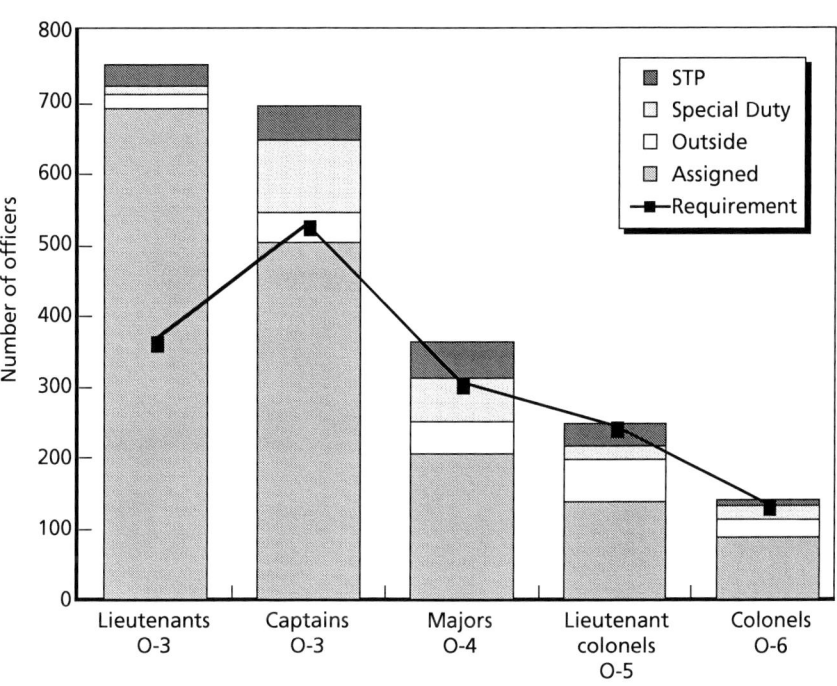

RAND MG131-3.11

field is exporting officers to other occupations and experiencing shortfalls that are caused by these policies.

Figure 3.12 shows that the overall manning rate has been consistently strong for most of the past decade; however, the overmanning of lieutenants has consistently driven the manning success. In recent years, the manning rate for O-3 through O-6 has been only 78 percent. In 2003, only 68 and 58 percent of the personnel positions at major and lieutenant colonel were filled.

Figure 3.12
Percentage of Manned Personnel Duty Assignments,
by Fiscal Year (excludes STP assignments)

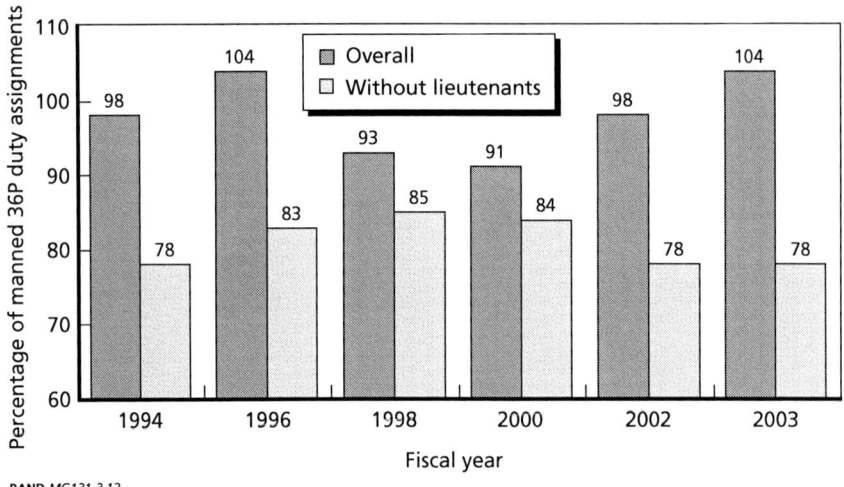

RAND *MG131-3.12*

The recent overmanning of lieutenants will not help with the major shortfall for almost another decade, unless promotion points[17] drop radically (although they have declined significantly in the Air Force as a whole). Another potential solution would be to reduce the flow of personnel officers to other career fields. The Air Force needs to weigh whether the demands outside the career field should continue to take precedence over filling positions within the field.

In addition to meeting requirements for mid-grade officers, personnel officers struggle to obtain appropriate experience to fill these positions. At the captain and major ranks, officers are selected to be Military Personnel Flight (MPF) commanders. In recent years, about 40 percent of potential candidates for these positions have had no previous experience working in MPFs. This "experience gap" occurs

---

[17] *Promotion points* are the nominal years of service at which promotions normally occur. If the promotion point for the transition from captain to major drops, new majors will have fewer years of service than previously.

because most of the junior-level positions are as squadron section commanders. The challenge is to provide young officers with some experience in MPFs so that they understand the full dimensions of personnel work while still filling the requirements for personnel officers in other parts of the organization.

Personnel officers are managed through the Directorate for Learning and Force Management in the office of the Deputy Chief of Staff for Personnel (AF/DPLF). The assignment team at AFPC is responsible for making assignments from the core of personnel officers, but they have little direct influence on accessions into the field. Some officers with other AFSCs fill personnel positions, but there is little flow from other career fields into personnel (unlike, for example, the flow of scientists and engineer into acquisition management). Most AFSCs are reluctant to lose officers (many other career fields are undermanned) to the nominally overfilled career field of personnel.

From the perspective of the assignment team, there are two main problems in managing personnel assignments. First, there is a high "tax" for special-duty jobs that requires them to place personnel officers into assignments in other career fields. For example, personnel officers are frequently picked for executive officer and instructor positions, as well as for other nonpersonnel positions. The assignment teams recognize the value of these assignments for broadening individual officers, but these assignments do limit flexibility in filling personnel positions.

Second, the personnel field has difficulty finding the right mix of company-grade assignments that provide career breadth and key experience in basic personnel skills. Personnel officers have good opportunities for assignments outside personnel, but these assignments sometimes limit the personnel-specific experience that is needed for mid-grade assignments.

From our interviews, we found that individuals who manage the personnel field make little use of analysis, again primarily because the field is seen as overstrength and therefore nominally healthy.

Force Management Perspective

The personnel career field does face some problems. In tactical management, there is some question about whether young lieutenants in personnel will stay in the Air Force. The overmanning of lieutenants implies that they are not sufficiently mentored. In addition, the structure of requirements in personnel means that many young officers must fill squadron section commander positions in which their exposure to key personnel experience is limited.

Operationally, the excess of lieutenants allows the field to satisfy the overall requirements for personnel, but the grade mix is not balanced. The current shortage of captains and majors is largely perceived as a short-term problem, but it is a problem that depends on lieutenant retention.

Finally, the management team in personnel must also confront the problem of personnel positions being left vacant while the officers fill needed positions in other fields. These assignments "out of core" come at some cost, and it is unclear who in the current management system decides whether that cost is too high. This decision is a strategic one that must be made above the level of the career field.

Communications and Information

The communications and information career field (33S) is focused on supporting and implementing joint and Air Force communications and information requirements across the service. In 2002, over 4,000 officers were assigned to communications jobs, and more than one-third of those officers were lieutenants. This career field has seen a myriad of retention issues during the past decade, mostly attributed to the period's strong economy in the information technology (IT) sector.

The communications field comprises many different technical skills. Responsibilities can vary from conducting offensive or defensive warfighting information operations, to managing systems networks, to programming computers, to managing visual information needs at the Air Staff. Relative to the private sector, it is not likely that one would find a job series that is collectively responsible for such a diverse set of tasks. Although one might find a network administrator responsible for establishing a network, this individual would not be lumped for purposes of career management with computer programmers and people responsible for the organization's audio-visuals needs.

Part of this career field's complexity may be attributed to the constantly evolving and growing area of IT activities within the Air Force. Such activities are found in such operational capabilities as information operations and in support mechanisms for the methods by which warfighters operate, such as the need for capable IT and communications systems to support most other functions.

For entry into the field, an officer must have an undergraduate degree with a minimum of 18 credit hours of IT-related courses (e.g., telecommunications, computers, mathematics, engineering, physics, information systems management, and information resources management). As noted earlier, an electrical engineering graduate could also serve as in this career field.[18]

To be designated a communications officer, an officer must complete the three-month Basic Communications and Information Officer Training (BCOT) course at Keesler AFB, Mississippi. Most communications officers attend this course upon commissioning. After BCOT, new lieutenants participate in the field-unique Aerospace Communications and Information Expertise (ACE) program, which places newly commissioned officers into an operationally related assignment. The ACE program lasts approximately two to three years during which each officer typically serves in base-level communications units as well as MAJCOM-level communications groups, combat communication units, combat camera units, and air communications squadrons.

After their ACE tour, officers typically transition to an intermediate staff job. Officers in these roles are usually involved in policy

---

[18] Officers with electrical engineering or computer engineering degrees are coded with an "A" suffix on the AFSC, (i.e., 33SxA).

development or program oversight. These officers usually have completed the Advanced Communications and Information Officer Training (ACOT) course at Keesler.

Understrength Problems

This career field meets its end-strength requirements with infusions of lieutenants. As Figure 3.13 shows, about 3.5 times more lieutenants are assigned than are required, which creates problems for the assignment teams in finding suitable positions and experience for hundreds of the "extra" young lieutenants. In addition, many of these

Figure 3.13
Assignment Patterns in Communications

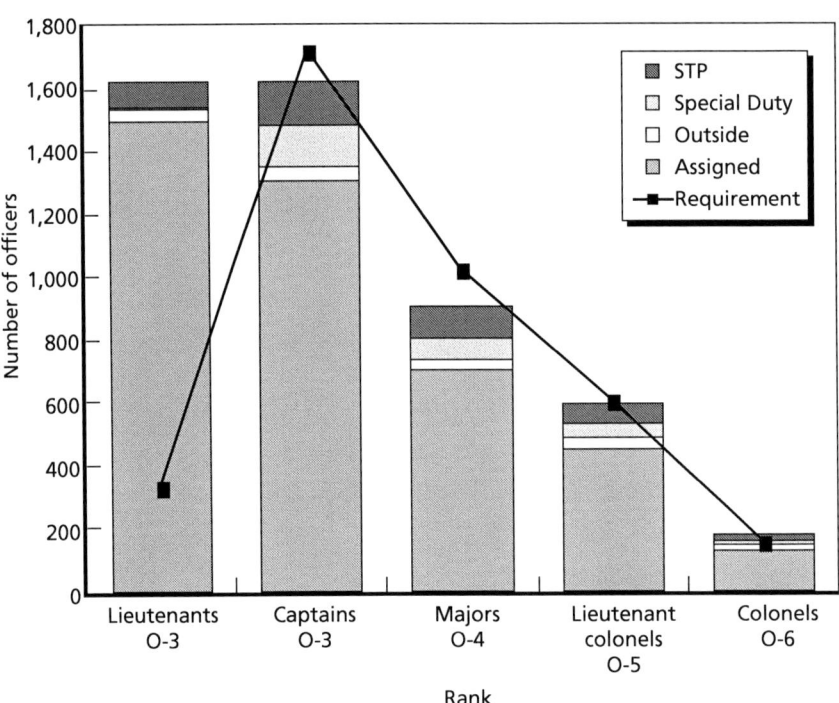

lieutenants may be poorly matched with their assignment or frustrated by jobs that either underutilize their skills or require greater experience levels than they possess.

The field is short of captains and field-grade officers. The share of officers in special-duty and outside assignments is smaller than for personnel, for example, but shortages would remain even if these officers were returned to communications assignments.

Figure 3.13 also shows an unsustainable requirement of 1,715 slots for captains relative to that of 329 for lieutenants. Even with little or no attrition from each accession cohort, the 5:1 ratio of captains to lieutenants is not sustainable. A ratio of 2:1 is considered sustainable.[19] If the career field is ever to meet its requirements at the captain level, then it needs to build a broader base of suitable lieutenant billets that will prepare more young officers for the captain positions. Building such a broad base would require some reengineering of the workplace for communications positions, either to provide more diverse experiences or possibly to segment the career field. Overmanning at the lieutenant level does little to address the problem, unless lieutenants who are not matched against career-field billets are actually doing communications work.

As with many other career fields, the field faces the challenge of keeping officers through a full career. Figure 3.14 shows the historical relationship of requirements to filled positions for the grades of lieutenant through colonel. In recent years, communications has been nominally healthy, but the field has a large shortfall when we look beyond the lieutenants.

To fix this experience deficit, the Air Force has implemented retention programs to keep senior company-grade and field-grade officers, including eligibility for the "Critical Skills Retention Bonus" described above.

---

[19] As a rough rule of thumb, a person is a lieutenant for four years and a captain for eight, which works out to the sustainable ratio of captains to lieutenants of 2:1. Note that decreasing nominal promotion points will exacerbate the unsustainability.

Figure 3.14
Percentage of Manned Communications Duty Assignments,
by Fiscal Year (excludes STP assignments)

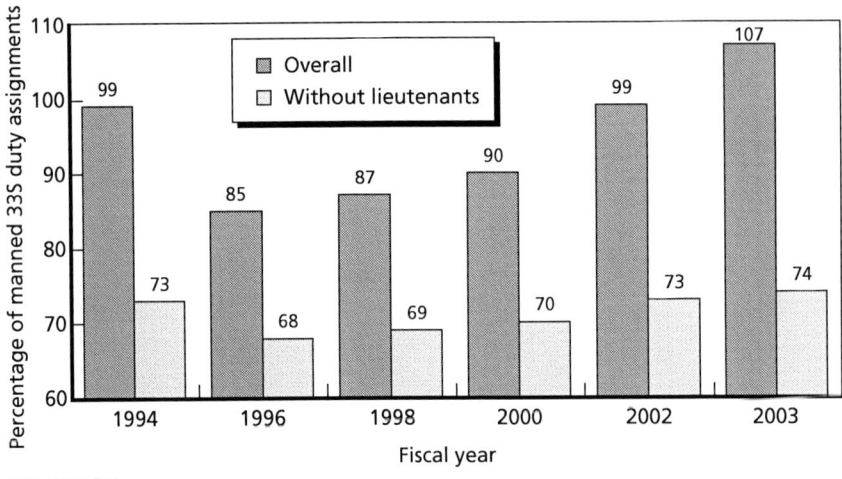

RAND MG131-3.14

Uniquely, the role of career field manager for this field is divided between two separate organizations within the Air Staff: the Directorate of Communications Operations in the office of the Deputy Chief of Staff for Installations and Logistics (AF/ILC) and the directorate for command, control, communications, and computers; intelligence, surveillance, and reconnaissance (C4ISR) infrastructure in the office of the Deputy Chief of Staff for Warfighting Integration (AF/XIC). AF/ILC is responsible for the management of members of the field who are more focused upon issues of base support; AF/XIC manages those who are involved with warfighting activities—i.e., offensive or defensive information operations. In light of the variety of skills associated with the occupation, this bifurcation is logical, although potentially cumbersome to coordinate. Interviews indicated that both two-letter Air Staff offices are involved with coordination and approval of development activities for this career field.

Force Management Perspective

The primary management challenge for this career field is operational: although the nominal health of the career field looks good, a closer look reveals important grade imbalances that have been due to retention issues such as the loss of officers to the private sector. This field has also had a substantial impact from the early retirement of prior-service officers who previously transferred from the enlisted to the officer corps after acquiring an IT background. The Air Force recently implemented a monetary bonus program to alleviate the retention problem, but as we noted in the section on acquisition managers, we found little analytic information about how the bonus was constructed or the effectiveness of the targeting.

There is another, tactical issue: Within the past decade, significant changes have occurred in the ratio of lieutenants to higher grades, with lieutenants now numbering over a third of all communications officers. As with other career fields overmanned with lieutenants, keeping these lieutenants occupied with interesting work that helps build their career skills presents a difficulty.

Intelligence

The intelligence career field (14N) incorporates a broad set of operations support functions. The field melds nine former subdivisions into a single AFSC and reflects AF policy to develop a "broadened specialist" with an understanding of intelligence beyond a specific technical area. The field expects officers to gain proficiency in four core competencies: (1) targeting, (2) intelligence, surveillance, and reconnaissance (ISR) battle planning, (3) unit/Air Operations Center (AOC), and (4) aerospace intelligence preparation of the battlespace/predictive battlespace analysis (AIPB/PBA).

The tension between broad and specific skills has important implications for intelligence officers' career paths. Officers are encouraged to master specific areas in their early assignments and then enter other areas to broaden their skills. Early assignments develop skills in one element, but several tours are needed for exposure to all elements of the core competencies. Even senior captains are unlikely to have exposure to every key component of the intelligence field. Ongoing assignment in a specific area is discouraged and hurts an officer's promotion prospects. Additionally, officers are strongly discouraged from serving back-to-back assignments outside the field, since doing so would allow their intelligence-related skills to atrophy.

Intelligence draws officers from a variety of backgrounds. The commissioning sources mirror those of all non-rated line officers: about 14 percent from USAFA, 50 percent from ROTC, and 36 percent from OTS. The vast majority of intelligence officers enter the field with nontechnical undergraduate degrees. In recent years, about 50 percent of officers have had social science majors and another 18 percent have majored in arts, humanities, and education.

Understrength Problems

As with communications officers, numerical requirements for entry-level intelligence officers are too low compared with the requirements for captains. Over the past eight years, the captain requirement has been about six times the requirement for lieutenants. For example, the requirement for captains in 2002 was 1,200, and the requirement for lieutenants was 200. This lopsided requirement structure creates severe manning problems in intelligence because the only path for growing intelligence captains is by developing intelligence lieutenants. With few lieutenant billets, the intelligence field managers have consistent problems in meeting the demand for captains.

Although there are few formal intelligence billets for lieutenants, the overmanning of lieutenant billets is critical for the overall manning position of the career field. Figure 3.15 shows that assigned strength is consistently less than the requirement for each grade above lieutenant. In reality, however, the extra lieutenants do fill some of the empty billets at the higher grades.

As Figure 3.15 shows, few company-grade officers have duty assignments outside the intelligence career field. Most captains assigned outside the career field work as instructors, and smaller numbers work as foreign area attachés, AF operations staff officers, or interna-

Figure 3.15
Assignment Patterns in Intelligence

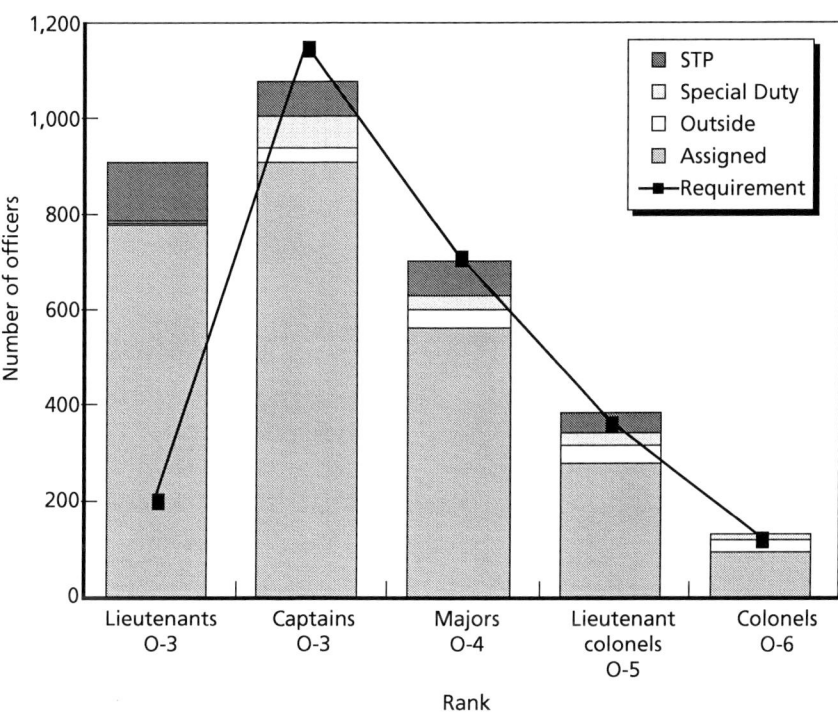

RAND *MG131-3.15*

tional politico-military affairs officers. Majors and lieutenant colonels are more likely to have assignments in operations support, whereas some lieutenant colonels take command responsibilities. Of intelligence colonels, 32 percent are assigned to positions outside the career field, with nearly half serving in command positions.

Intelligence work requires considerable specialized training and experience, so few intelligence assignments are filled by officers from outside the intelligence field. With little lateral entry, managing the career field depends critically on a steady flow of accessions, developing enough junior officers to meet the demand at higher ranks, and managing fluctuations in retention.

The ad hoc solution to the shortfall of captains has been to over-access lieutenants (i.e., access many more lieutenants than required) in the hopes of funneling more officers into the captain ranks. The problem with this strategy is that the Air Force has few lieutenant intelligence billets, which presumably limits officers' opportunities to gain suitable entry-level intelligence experience. In addition, as we have noted with the preceding career fields, lieutenants may become disenchanted with poor assignment and development opportunities, thereby becoming less likely to remain in the Air Force as captains when their initial service obligation ends.

Why does the requirement for captains dwarf that for lieutenants? Intelligence officers have an extended training and development process, so lieutenants are considered not suitable for many assignments. The MAJCOMs and other organizations employing intelligence officers believe that an intelligence officer needs a range of experience in intelligence assignments to fulfill their requirements. In addition, company-grade intelligence officers are often assigned to small, isolated work groups, so it is difficult to divide the work between lieutenants and captains. In larger work groups, there are greater opportunities for more-experienced personnel to mentor lieutenants and for lieutenants to gain proficiency.[20]

Figure 3.16 shows that overall manning in intelligence has been consistently strong (over 90 percent for the past decade), but this manning success is driven by overmanning of lieutenants. The manning results for captains and field-grade officers are much less positive, with manning levels hovering at about 75 percent. The long-run hope is that the overmanning of lieutenants will eventually translate into better manning at the captain and field-grade levels—a hope that seems unrealistic, considering that the overmanning of lieutenant slots in the mid-1990s has not alleviated the shortfalls in captains and field-grade intelligence officers in the early 2000s.

---

[20] Interestingly, the Navy has a similar unsustainable grade structure for its intelligence officers (Thie et al., 2003).

Figure 3.16
Percentage of Manned Intelligence Duty Assignments,
by Fiscal Year (excludes STP assignments)

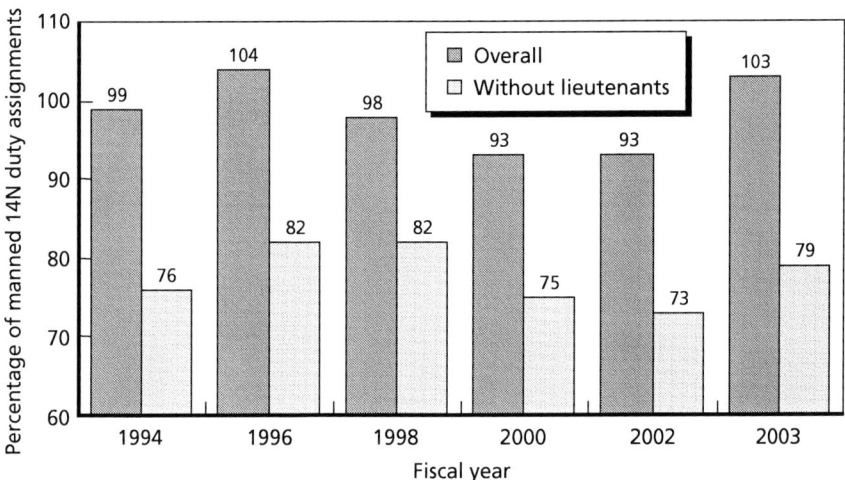

RAND *MG131-3.16*

Intelligence officers are managed through the Director of Intelligence, Surveillance, and Reconnaissance in the office of the Deputy Chief of Staff for Air and Space Operations at the Air Staff (AF/XOI). This office houses the career field manager for intelligence as well as the control over training and education programs for the field. The CFM coordinates with MAJCOMs and joint commands to collect requirement information. (The intelligence community includes a large share of joint command assignments relative to other fields, which complicates requirements determination.)

The linkages between AF/DP and AF/XOI are perceived as being not well defined. Some personnel issues (e.g., accessions and bonuses) are managed by the personnel community; others are handled through the CFM. In some cases, communication and decisionmaking between the two groups has been disjointed. However, with the CFM position only recently becoming full-time, the coordination of tasks between the intelligence and personnel organizations is improving. This change has also allowed the CFM to take a more active role in pressing intelligence personnel issues at the

Air Staff and starting to develop an in-house capability for analyzing personnel issues.

The assignment team struggles with the long pipeline for developing intelligence officers. After the initial seven months of entry-level training, an intelligence officer requires another 18 months of experience to become nominally a fully qualified intelligence officer. However, the young officers are still not suitably prepared for many assignments, and this leaves the assignment officers with a long stretch when the young officers count against strength but cannot be assigned to all slots. Since there are few lieutenant billets, the assignment teams continue to try to convince MAJCOMs to take more lieutenants.

Force Management Perspective

The ongoing challenge for managing intelligence officers is both tactical and operational. At the tactical level, the career path for intelligence officers needs to be rethought at the most junior levels. The solution would seem to lie in efforts to shift some billets from captain to lieutenant positions. Such shifting would entail working with the MAJCOMs and joint agencies to define more-suitable work for lieutenants. Positions should be designed so that younger officers could be mentored by more-experienced intelligence officers and gain valuable experience while contributing to the mission. Where feasible, AF intelligence organizations should consider realigning work groups so that intelligence work would be consolidated for a group of officers within which mentoring could take place.

From an operational standpoint, the unsustainable requirements for lieutenants and captains need to be fixed. The overmanning of lieutenant positions is not a suitable fix for this problem, for two reasons. First, extra lieutenants have not historically grown the pool of captains to meet requirements. Second, with few lieutenant billets, the career field is hard-pressed to find suitable intelligence experience for the lieutenants that are available.

Implications of the Case Studies

This in-depth review of the career fields revealed chronic manning problems for non-rated line officers. The Air Force has attracted enough young lieutenants to meet overall end-strength requirements in four of these fields, but severe problems exist in meeting grade-level requirements. These problems are not new to the Air Force. Our interviews and historical data show that shortages of O-3 through O-6 personnel have been common for the past decade. Our discussions with assignment teams and CFMs suggested that these managers hoped that the overmanning of lieutenant positions would help solve these shortages as new cohorts moved through the system. However, in recent years, the Air Force has consistently overmanned lieutenant positions, and this practice has done little to stem problems in manning captain and field-grade shortages. From anecdotes, we can say that some of this failure can be attributed to loss of junior officers because of what they perceive are unchallenging jobs and unattractive career paths.

The case studies reveal that most career field management activity concentrates on day-to-day, or tactical, decisions. Assignment teams and CFMs focus on matching "faces" to "spaces" in each assignment cycle. They must schedule education and training tours as well as find suitable assignments for career development. Assignment teams are also faced with the challenge of filling special-duty positions and finding career-broadening opportunities for officers outside their core AFS. Finally, most career fields have shortages in some grades, so the CFM must work with the MAJCOMs to negotiate a set of priorities for rationing available officers across required positions. These short-term problems are formidable and leave little time for operational-level issues of career-field health.

Several key operational and strategic issues receive inadequate attention in the current management scheme, and these issues limit the effectiveness of officer management and development. The problems are not temporary, and they are not being effectively addressed through current Air Force management channels:

- Grade imbalances. Each of the case studies showed problems in meeting some, if not most, of the O-3 through O-6 grades.
- Sustainable requirement. Intelligence and communications-information officers have grade-requirement structures that are unsustainable. The lieutenant and captain requirements are severely out of alignment: too few requirements for lieutenants to sustain the requirements for captains. A management decision is needed to reengineer these requirements in some manner.
- Skill development. In several occupations, officer duties are too isolated to allow proper development. For example, intelligence tasks need to be redesigned so that the surplus of lieutenants can be used to lessen the shortage of captains. In the personnel field, squadron section commander positions provide limited background in job content for mid-grade positions in MPFs and also are isolated from other personnel jobs.
- Narrow or inaccurate requirement. Many acquisition jobs require an officer with an engineering background. Along with promotion rates of acquisition officers, this requirement helps explain the assignment of engineers to acquisition. However, the classification of such a job as an acquisition job means that EE requirements are, if anything, understated. Conversely, some acquisition jobs have reportedly been reclassified as engineering jobs because such slots have a higher priority for assignments.
- Priorities for special-duty and outside assignments. In many cases, assignment teams fill these outside positions while positions remain vacant in an officer's trained skill. While it may be argued that some of these jobs are more important to the Air Force than having officers in their core area, the quotas on each career field are often leveled on a pro-rata basis, with each field contributing proportionally, instead of making decisions based on importance of unfilled jobs. The Air Force should have some mechanism for weighing the importance of filling the special-duty or outside assignment against the vacancy that doing so creates in the officer's core AFS. In many cases, we found enough officers to fill grade-level requirements, but these officers

were systematically dispatched to assignments outside their career fields.

- While accession levels are high in most career fields, the Air Force faces a problem in attracting engineers. The share of new non-rated line officers that is engineers and electrical engineers has declined substantially since 1999. This shortage of engineering entrants has important implications for Air Force manning of technical occupations for years to come.

As we have pointed out, many, if not most, of these problems are known to CFMs and assignment teams. Further, recent studies such as the TFCFR highlighted many of these problems. The fundamental problem is that the people who have the insight do not have access to such policy levers as accessions policy, bonus policy, and design of career paths and jobs to help solve the problem. The underlying problem is that the Air Force does not have strong management institutions at the operational and strategic levels to address the fundamental causes of the understrength issues we have highlighted. We discuss these institutions in the next chapter.

CHAPTER FOUR

Force Management in the Air Force: Challenges, History, and Current Initiatives

As we indicated in Chapter Three, several key findings resulted from the case studies of the five career fields. Although these findings were highlighted with respect to the career fields chosen for the study, our data analyses and discussions with assignment teams, CFMs, and members of the AF/DP staff indicate that these same challenges exist across other Air Force specialties as well.

Tactical Success Versus Operational and Strategic Challenges

Guided by the framework presented in Chapter Two and our interpretation of the case studies in Chapter Three, we contend that the Air Force does well at the tactical level of force management, particularly in the next-assignment process. On a daily basis, assignment officers do an effective job of executing assignment actions. However, tactical measures of effectiveness, such as position fill rates and time to fill positions, tend to drive assignment processes that emphasize the near term: a goal of filling spaces quickly and drawing only from the current pool of officers up for reassignment.

This process does not necessarily result in optimal career paths for the officers or the institution. In fact, there are considerable disconnects and gaps in operational- and strategic-level force management. This is where the policies must be set to address the root causes of understrength problems, such as imbalances in accessions, retention, and grades.

As an example of this gap, during FY2002–2003, the Air Force accessed more second lieutenants than required, but it did not target the accessions in a manner that addressed some of the critical, identified shortages. Instead of accessing more electrical engineers through targeted recruiting and/or scholarships, the accessions sources brought in an abundance of support officers in nontechnical career fields such as business and liberal arts, who were then placed into such career fields as intelligence and personnel. Our discussions indicated that the process for determining how many of what type majors were accessed was not well connected to requirements. Accessing more nontechnical officers than demanded has at least two consequences for the future management of the officer corps: (1) Electrical engineers will continue to be understrength relative to requirements within at least the near term, and (2) other nontechnical career fields will have a surplus of lieutenants compared with the individual requirements of non-EE career fields. Not only has one problem not been resolved, but another problem has been created.

The underrecruitment of such technical specialties as electrical engineering, coupled with the overrecruitment of nontechnical officers, indicates a process that is not linked to other parts of the force management process. From an operational perspective, the measure of health of a career field or family of career fields should drive the near-term and longer-term accession requirements. At the strategic level, the linkage of accessions to future demands (such as officers with specialized academic majors that may not exist today) is not well vetted within the current framework.

From an operational and strategic perspective, the Air Force has not constructed processes or measures to assess how well the supply of officer competencies match the demand for such competencies (in our assessment, an operational task) or whether there are actions that can be taken to ensure the optimal balance of career fields across the entire officer corps: a more strategic activity that examines the supply versus demand of occupational requirements across the Air Force.

How Has the Air Force Evolved to this Current State?

Given this track record of mixed effectiveness (tactical hits in the context of operational and strategic misses), one may wonder how and why the Air Force has evolved to this place today. The Appendix describes many reasons: the drawdown of the force, the elimination or reduction of analytic functions focused on force management, and the use of the all-volunteer assignment system (largely allowing each officer to select his/her next assignment) during the early 1990s.

Another explanation for the current situation is that the Air Force is oriented toward tactical activities because of the continuous near-term pressures it is under to "get things done," coupled with an organizational culture that emphasizes a decentralized approach toward achievement of objectives. The force drawdown of the 1990s has only exacerbated this phenomenon by requiring the service to "do more with less." In the context of Air Force activities, most of the "more" has been focused on getting the day-to-day tasks accomplished, as opposed to considering the optimization of activities at either the operational or strategic level. The symptoms that we observed in the case studies were indicative of this focus as well: Many of the issues exist because of a lack of operational or strategic orientation, which, in many cases, requires a stronger, centralized approach toward force management. This approach also requires stronger linkages across organizations that affect the success of force management.

A final reason for the issues that we observed is how the organization is structured from a functional perspective. As our colleague Carl Builder pointed out in his work *The Icarus Syndrome* (Builder, 1994), Air Force officers tend to associate with their functional orientation (fighter pilot, meteorologist, logistician, engineer, etc.), to the point that they define their identity as what they are (functionally speaking) as opposed to their profession (military officer). Accordingly, the institution has tended to manage officers within functional areas.

Managing the officer corps exclusively by functional orientation is limited in that there will be less strategic vision across the entire institution. The types of examples that we found in the case studies were indicative of this strategic and operational suboptimization. Further, the functionals tend to focus on tactical activities because of the nature of this stovepiping and because many of the CFM roles tend to be part-time, additional duties. This status does not allow the CFM much time or energy to focus on broader, long-term issues that may affect the whole career field (the operational level) or the entire force (strategic level). Likewise, a part-time focus does not lend itself toward the development or use of analyses that would address the operational or strategic issues.

Similarly to the AFPC assignment teams, the CFM tends to place his/her focus on activities that are very much oriented day to day rather than having a farther reach and influencing longer-term objectives. Some career fields have recently re-established full-time CFMs, particularly in the new force management initiative described in the next section, and have begun to use analytic methods to assess career-field health.

Current USAF Force Management Initiatives

The USAF personnel community has not been idle in the area of force management; on the contrary, the past few years have seen a number of initiatives and programs that address various aspects of what we have termed *force management*. We describe here the major efforts and how they relate to our research. We must note, however, that at the time of writing (late 2003), the force management environment was changing rapidly. Hence, our description will necessarily be of only part of what is happening.

Revised Authorization Initiative
One of our major assumptions was that the requirement—the authorizations in each career field—was a valid estimate of manpower needs in that field. This assumption is widely disputed, as we acknowledged, both by manpower people in the Air Force and by outside researchers. However, the Air Force has been embarked on a "balance-the-books" effort to refine the requirements for each career

field and to keep them current. Of the five case-study career fields presented here, all were understrength in total numbers when our research began in 2002. When the authorizations were revised, in the third quarter of 2003, four of the five fields were nominally overstrength, due partially to changes in authorizations (as we noted above, overaccession of lieutenants distorts that picture). This initiative needs to be pursued aggressively because, without credible requirements, it is impossible to assess shortfalls and overages credibly. However, the new requirements do not appear to have been tested against such criteria as whether they are sustainable (the intelligence requirements were still unsustainable).

Air Force Senior Leader Management Office

Another development has been the establishment of the Air Force Senior Leader Management Office (AFSLMO). This office aims to define career paths for promising Air Force personnel, both uniformed and civilian. The career paths will give such personnel the experiences they need in order to assume senior leader positions in the service as general officers and civilian senior executives.

Unfortunately, this is what we would term a tactical-level management effort, although aimed at developing personnel with leadership capabilities that span the entire Air Force, not just a single career field.

Three Publications on Development

As of this writing, several of the topics we have addressed are the subject of three closely related efforts: the Chief's Sight Pictures on Force Development (U.S. Air Force, 2003b–d), the United States Air Force Strategic Personnel Plan (U.S. Air Force, 2004), and the draft 36-series AFI on Force Development (U.S. Air Force, 2003e).

The three publications use a slightly different definition of *development*. The Strategic Plan (U.S. Air Force, 2004) has three central sets of processes that cover all aspects of direct personnel management—sustain, renew and develop—and the last of the three aspects is focused on the education, training, and career management of individual Air Force personnel. The other two documents, particularly the AFI, define *force development* as the overarching shaping and maintenance of the Air Force workforce, the processes we have labeled *force management.* In the body of the AFI, references are made to force management as being contained in force development.[1]

In our opinion, these differences are semantic.[2] There is broad general agreement on the processes that must be performed, and the designation of the collection of processes as force development or force management seems to be purely a definitional issue.

However, much of the focus has been at the tactical level—i.e., the career paths and assignments of individual officers—particularly in the Chief's Sight Pictures, at least in the sense that they focus on the much closer attention that the USAF will give to an individual's sequence of assignments and education. This focus is to be expected from a short communication aimed at each individual member of the workforce. However, implicit in such a focus are strong operational and strategic (in our sense) planning and guidance to define these career paths and monitor the evolution of the workforce structure.

The new AFI and the Strategic Plan pay more attention to all three levels of force management/development although they do not use this precise terminology. One of the major new organizations is the development team to provide career path planning and monitoring for individual officers—the missing part of current tactical force management. Further, the assignment process, which is strong already, will be linked with the development team by the presence of assignment team members on the development team.

At the strategic level, the AFI and the Strategic Plan envision that strategic force management or force development will be the responsibility of a Force Development Council (FDC), chaired by the AF Vice Chief, and including senior representation from MAJCOMs and other appropriate Air Force organizations. It will have a staff or-

---

[1] A volume on force development also is in draft form in the Air Force Doctrine series.

[2] Although there are human resource researchers who assert that development pertains only to the training and education, in the broadest sense, of individuals.

ganization in DP, the Force Development Office (FDO), and an analytic organization, the Force Development Support Office (FDSO). One of the tasks of FDSO will be to support the FDO. This strategic-level organization tracks closely with the vision of the required strategic force management structure we present in Chapter Five.[3] However, as of this writing, none of these strategic force management organizations is in existence. In contrast, the development teams have started meeting, setting up procedures, and looking at officer records.

It is at the operational force management level that the structures are particularly vague. The AFI (and earlier briefings) identified one of the primary tasks of the development teams as the maintenance of the "health of the career field," which seems to include ongoing analyses such as those done for the TFCFR. However, we encountered other opinions as to how the development teams would function in practice—for example, that most career-field decisions would be made by the FDO with "advice" from the development teams.

Given the development teams' virtual nature,[4] and the workload they face just in reviewing all of the relevant personnel in a given career field, we have doubts as to how much sustained attention they can give to detailed diagnoses and analyses of career-field health. In particular, it is not clear to what extent they will be able to use the services of the FDSO and whether the FDSO will be adequately staffed to meet their needs as well as those of the FDO. This is troubling, because our research indicates that operational-level force management is key: It provides the structure for tactical management and the basic information for strategic management. However, its place is not yet clear in the current organizations envisioned in "force development."

---

[3] We should note that some senior members of the AF personnel community have suggested that the FDC role should be assumed directly by the AF council in its general role as the final arbiter for AF resource allocation decisions.

[4] It is expected that they will meet regularly to do their work, but they will not be a standing organization.

As to analytic support, AF/DP is supporting the development of the Total Human Resources Management Information System (THRMIS), which is an information system designed to bring aggregate personnel data to the desktop of CFMs and other members of the personnel community. Currently it primarily extracts and displays descriptive data. The addition of modeling capability is being considered, but the question of how expert support will be provided to use such models (which can be complex) is still being debated.

Who Will Do Operational-Level Management?

One final issue of force management needs to be addressed: Who will do the operational-level management for AF leaders, the focus of AFSLMO's work? At some point in an officer's career, he or she is recognized as a candidate for a senior leadership role, at which point his/her career development switches from purely career field to adding experiences relevant to developing senior leaders. As with all officers, there is a tactical-level function to be performed, and there will need to be coordination with the initial career field management so that appropriate assignments can be provided.

CHAPTER FIVE

Conclusions and Recommendations

Our original goal was to examine the causes of chronic understrength conditions in Air Force career fields and to determine which were systemic and which were tied to specific situations in individual career fields. We have argued in this report that many aspects of the understrength problem are due to the lack of operational-level and strategic-level career-field management in the Air Force. While this lack does not cause some of the problems, such as private-sector competition, it does inhibit diagnosis and the formulation of effective responses across the service.

Without monitoring, analysis, and action at the strategic and operational levels, tactical-level management (working with the assignment of individual officers) has neither the access to effective policy levers nor the career field–wide information to effectively deal with understrength problems. Such problems require authority and decisions on accessions, career paths, requirements determination, retention monitoring and control, and other policy areas. Further, since Air Force resources are limited, some decisions on allocation of those resources across career fields (such as the mix of active, Guard/Reserve, civilian, and contractor personnel) must be made above the level of individual career field manager. In the preceding chapter, we discussed reasons why these gaps currently exist. In the rest of this chapter, we discuss what needs to be done to close the gaps.

Reinstituting Force Management

Doing the Operational Job

Operational-level force management, the management of career fields or career-field families, is the key to force management as a whole. It provides the policy framework that guides tactical-level management: policies on career paths, education and training, and cross-flow and career-broadening opportunities. These policies must be in place for development teams and assignment officers to help officers plan their careers in both the short and long terms. Operational-level management also provides the basic informational input for strategic-level decisions: It provides the first level of oversight to detect and diagnose problems in a career field, and its familiarity with the field makes it the primary source of potential actions to fix problems.

Operational-level management requires two major and distinct skill sets:

1. Substantive knowledge of the career field
2. Knowledge of how to manage a dynamic, closed, hierarchical personnel system.

The first skill set is the basis of the current operational-level management structure of functional CFMs. The second skill set is one that is generic across career fields. It requires analytic insight and an appreciation of how the interplay between accessions, differential retention, and inflows and outflows affect career fields' strength, overall and by grade in a personnel system in which senior people must be developed from junior personnel. The dynamic, multiyear character of management is hard to appreciate without analytic training and experience using models to explore the effects of specified personnel policies. This latter skill set is generally missing in operational-level management: Most CFMs are not analysts. Further, currently they have little access to this type of analytic assistance.

Doing the Strategic Job

The strategic management job is the most difficult one, but it is the most important for the long-term health of the force. Essentially, this job is the locus at which resources are balanced so that the Air Force has the balanced force it needs, where *balance* is referred to in terms of skills, experience levels, and types of workers. This balancing act sometimes requires making explicit decisions about which career fields get resources, such as bonus payments, and demonstrating a willingness to make and accept trade-offs among career fields in order to optimize the overall mission-readiness of the force.

The strategic level also must oversee the operational-level management, ensuring that problems are handled adequately by that level and are not being ignored or deferred.

As with the operational level, this level also requires analytic support, which should be capable of both operational-level analysis and total-force analysis.

The strategic level must also have the high-level authority to make and enforce forcewide decisions on all of the strategic personnel issues. Simply rolling up and aggregating operational-level decisions is not adequate for maintaining a balanced force.

Doing the Tactical Job

One-half of tactical-level management has a good process in place: The next-assignment process has been set up and refined to handle the cyclic nature of the assignment cycle efficiently and with maximal attention to both the individual officers' requests and the needs of the service (given current staffing as of early 2003). However, RAND researchers found in a study of the space career field (AFS 13S; Vernez et al., unpublished) that operational-level information on job-experience requirements was not being provided to assignment officers, leading to problems matching people with jobs.

The other half of tactical-level management is defining long-term career goals and plans for individual officers and helping them to follow those plans and achieve those goals.

How to Do the Job

Operational Level

Make the CFM a full-time position, and put a senior functional officer in the position. Operational-level management requires a senior person to take responsibility for monitoring the state of each career field (or career-field family, depending on size). Given the requirement for functional expertise to understand professional issues, as well as the need for credibility in the career field and with the general officers responsible for policy in that professional area, this position should be a CFM-type position filled by a senior officer, preferably an O-6 or senior O-5, or possibly a senior civilian. This position would have access and input to accessions management, retention policy decisions, cross-flow and career-broadening policies, and promotion performance for the field.

In view of these responsibilities, it seems clear that most CFMs should be located at the Air Staff so that they can provide inputs to policy formulation. This location allows close contact with the staffs setting policy for each career field, as well as with the personnel community.

Provide the CFMs with dedicated and standardized analytic support. In addition, the CFM must have access to analytic capability that can address the complex technical personnel issues involved in managing the field. Such capability must include modeling of the evolution of the workforce under different policies. This capability would go beyond the current modeling available to include, for example, econometric modeling of bonus and promotion policies.[1]

At least two basic options present themselves for organizing the CFM and analytic capabilities for operational-level management:

---

[1] See, for example, Ausink et al. (2003) for examples of this type of analysis. In the draft AFI on force development (U.S. Air Force, 2001b), the FDSO is supposed to provide this support; however, current plans call for the FDSO to be located at AFPC in San Antonio, not at the Air Staff, and the FDSO is also slated to support the FDO. Whether it will have enough personnel to do both of these jobs remains to be seen.

1. Consolidate the CFMs in an Air Staff operational management organization. DP would provide analytic capability. This arrangement has the advantage of facilitating collaboration between CFMs in working on general career field management issues while maintaining their positions as managers, monitors, and advocates for their career fields. One concern is the issue of their relationship with the senior officers in their career field. An alternative is to have a dual reporting chain (to AF/DP and to their functional career-field leader); given the level of responsibility, this dual chain would certainly be necessary for credibility and effectiveness. (The model here is AFPC, where assignments are made by functionals who formally work for DP but have strong attachments to their functional community leadership; personnel technicians provide the infrastructure.)
2. Leave the CFMs in their functional organizations as now, and assign DP-provided analytic capability to them in a matrix fashion.[2] Some career fields may be large enough to warrant full-time analysts; others may be grouped for analytic purposes.

It is important to emphasize that, in both options, while the analytic support would work for the CFMs, it would use analytic tools, models, data, and practices that are standardized across all functional communities. This commonality is necessary for minimizing discrepancies in policy advocacy caused by differing data definitions and assumptions, as well as for providing cost efficiencies.

Strategic Level

Establish strategic-level personnel decisionmaking in a senior body with authority to make decisions for the Air Force. The high level of decisionmaking required for strategic-level management (making forcewide decisions) may require two different organizations. The decisionmaking function should reside in a body of high-ranking

---

[2] Analysts would be trained by DP and would use centrally maintained databases, but they would be assigned to an individual CFM to provide dedicated analytic support to the management of that particular career field.

officers and senior civilians who can make wide-ranging and potentially controversial (e.g., shifting jobs between the active force and the reserves) personnel decisions for the Air Force as a whole. Such a body probably would be chaired by a senior general officer or a senior civilian from the Air Force Secretariat, and have representation from the Air Staff, the MAJCOMs, and the Secretariat offices. The Force Development Council envisioned in the draft AFI on force development (U.S. Air Force, 2003b) has this level of authority, although it has been suggested by some that the Air Force Council should add force management to their current responsibilities as arbiter of service resources.

Provide the strategic-level decisionmaking body with a full-time staff. However, such a body clearly cannot carry out the routine activities required to implement strategic management: monitoring operational-level management, formulating and directing analyses on management options, etc. The decisionmaking body will therefore need a staff/analytic office to support its personnel responsibilities. Although this body should be independent of the CFMs, it will need to work closely with them. Its analytic capabilities will need to be consistent with those used at the operational level—i.e., the analysts should be colleagues, and the data and tools should be common both to this staff and to the CFMs' analysts, subject to the special needs of strategic-level analysis (e.g., different models may need to be used with higher levels of aggregation for strategic-level decisionmaking).

As with the operational-level analysis capability, this staffing probably should be a DP organization. The Force Development Office envisioned in the draft AFI would meet this need. However, its role in strategic-level management is currently vague.

Tactical Level

Provide development teams and assignment teams with clear operational- and strategic-level guidance for managing individual careers and making assignments. The AFPC assignment teams seem to be well suited to handle next assignments (provided, as noted above, that they are given operational-level guidance such as complete job requirements). This is a big enough job without their having to deal with the operational-level issues that different teams have had to take on and deal with in the past.

The new development teams being formed in different career areas also seem to be the right organizational location for the longer-term tactical-level management (career paths for individual officers). Run by the CFM (and in this concept as well, the CFM is a more senior position than it is currently) and chaired by the functional manager (a GO), this team has the visibility and continuity to provide this level of management.[3] However, as with the next-assignment function, these tasks require operational- and strategic-level policymaking to provide a good framework for advising officers on their individual careers.

Future Research

Our case studies focused on non-rated line officers for the reasons cited in Chapter Three. However, we argue that our conclusions about the need for enhanced operational and strategic management applies also to rated officers, the enlisted force, and to the Guard/Reserve, civilian, and contractor segments of the operational and support workforce. Because the Air Force mission of projecting aerospace power requires a workforce with a broad mix of skills and experience levels, that force must be managed at the strategic level, and attention must be given to more detail than just numbers for end strength and overall grade distribution.

How operational-level management structures should be ar-ranged is an open question, however. The current CFM for scientists and engineers (SAF/AQRE) has responsibility for both officers and civilians. But the very diversity of career fields, training requirements, concentration in active as opposed to Guard/Reserve, and the relative numbers of officers and enlisted might require that operational-level management be somewhat different across the career fields. For

---

[3] Examples of this kind of general guidance include publications such as the *Career Development Guide for Scientists and Engineers* (U.S. Air Force, 2003a).

example, the field of computer support operations (base networks, and hardware and software support and training) might be best managed jointly for officers and enlisted personnel, whereas areas such as logistics might be better separated.

This report has also emphasized the necessity of analytic tools at the operational level for monitoring the health of career fields and projecting the effects of different management decisions over a number of years. Because most of the military career fields are hierarchical, closed systems, drops in accessions and/or retention problems can cause shortages in manning that persist for years, until new people can be brought in and work their way up. Managing such flows is not an intuitive skill; it requires experience and the use of models to get insight into the effects of proposed policies and to understand the long-term implications of those policies (Vernez et al., unpublished; Bigelow et al., 2003). It also requires consistent data and data definitions, as well as standardized background and training of analysts. It is unlikely that functionals will be able to fully develop this type of insight during their tours in a CFM office.

Management at the strategic level will also require substantial analysis. Some analysis will use operational-level methods (especially for oversight) or will involve straightforward aggregation of operational-level results. However, as the Air Force develops more experience with more comprehensive strategic management, other analytic needs may surface.

One of our reviewers noted that the force management framework we have argued for is not a panacea. The Air Force has had parts of a very similar framework before, as well as much more analytic capability for personnel issues than it has now (see the Appendix for more details), and managing the force as a closed, hierarchical system still proved a challenge for generations of intelligent and sophisticated personnel managers. And Air Force personnel management will always face exogenous constraints and challenges: the sudden appearance of new threats, budget shocks, new and obsolete career fields, and competition from a dynamic private sector. Even so, we argue that the best way to deal with these challenges is to have a three-tier management framework that can address issues at the individual, career-field, and forcewide level—and take appropriate actions at the right level.

Brief Historical Background of Force Management

To better understand today's force management environment and to provide a context for the present and for the road ahead, it is important to examine some of the history of Air Force force management. Force management in the Air Force over the past three decades—the composition of Air Force Personnel Center (AFPC) assignment teams and other AFPC and Air Staff organizations involved with the process, as well as the overall interaction/partnership between personnel managers with career-field functional managers (to the extent they existed)—can be characterized as ambivalent between centralization of information and decisions and the polar opposite of devolving most if not all decsionmaking to local commanders and the people under their command.

Pre–FY1992/1993 Force Drawdown

Before the fiscal year (FY)1992/1993 force drawdown, the Air Force's officer-assignment system had been relatively stable for over a decade. Its fundamental priorities were (1) mission requirements, (2) officer professional development, and (3) individual preference. Assignment policy was formulated at AFPC (the responsibility moved to the Air Staff around 1992), and assignment teams were invested with a great deal of authority in managing and distributing the force.

The assignment teams of that era (called PALACE Teams) were headed by senior lieutenant colonels who were handpicked by the leadership of the functional communities to perform what was widely recognized as a selective and prestigious job. This gave the Personnel Center (AFPC) in-house, respected career-field representatives who had strong links to the Air Staff to get things done. Other assignment team members were also strong functional representatives who served as "resource managers." Resource managers were charged not just with distributing the force but also with ensuring that officers got "the right next job"—i.e., managing the personnel resources of the Air Force.

In addition to the robust (i.e., experienced and highly competent) nature of the old PALACE Assignment Teams, AFPC also had a Force Management Branch during this era. Its charter was to perform the analytic "heavy lifting" to aid assignment teams and policy formulators, ensuring the healthy management of career fields across the board.

One should not assume, however, that this era had mastered force management. The officer-assignment system arguably allowed for fast decision cycles because both policymaking and analysis occurred in-house at AFPC. However, the system and supporting technology of the era allowed officers little, if any, visibility into the assignments that were coming available. Further, many officers and some commanders were frustrated by what they felt was their having too little voice in the system, in contrast to the authority they perceived as being invested in the assignment teams. This would change.

FY1992/1993 Drawdown

Taken in historical context, there is really nothing new about drawing down the strength of the Air Force or that of the military in general. A cursory look at post-World War II (WWII), post-Korea, post-Vietnam, and the post-Reagan era readily reveals this repeated cycle. In fact, in the period between 1988 and 1991, the Air Force had already drawn down the force by nearly 100,000, through attrition.

However, the FY1992/1993 force drawdown represents the most radical downsizing of the Air Force since the end of WWII.

Additionally, it was the first time the Air Force had to draw down an all-volunteer force. All Air Force personnel affected by this drawdown had volunteered to serve their country, many in recent combat, and they expected to be able to continue their service until retirement. Further, in the absence of a draft, drawdown programs could have negatively affected future recruitment efforts if they were perceived as biased or callous. For these reasons, great emphasis was placed on downsizing the volunteer force through volunteer programs and on ensuring that downsizing initiatives were conducted in the most equitable, objective manner possible, thereby preserving the dignity of quality personnel. Involuntary RIF (reduction in force) action was considered to be a last resort.

Against this backdrop, one can see that, while force-shaping considerations were central to planning and targeting various year-groups of officers (officers who entered together in a given year as a cohort) for drawdown programs, they were not always the driving consideration in drawdown decisions. This lack of primary emphasis on force shaping would have consequences both in the short term and in the future.

For example, in keeping with congressional guidelines for accomplishing Department of Defense (DoD) strength reductions, the first thing the Air Force did was to reduce accessions over a period of several years. Congressional guidelines next focused on retirement-eligible and first-term populations, and last, on departures from the rest of the force (voluntary first, involuntary last). This priority reflected the sensitivity to drawing down the career force in an all-volunteer military with corresponding future-retention concerns. But constraining accessions for several years below the levels needed to sustain the force created a shortage of people to fill requirements (colloquially called a "bathtub" because the shortage was localized to specific year-groups) of several year-groups. Constraining accessions for a period of years creates "bathtubs" in year-groups that move through the force for 20 years. While the bathtub effect created during the drawdown years has been well publicized in the rated community, not as much attention was paid to the non-rated officer community, which had similar accession constraints.

Since the bulk of the voluntary and involuntary drawdown programs targeted the non-rated force, the bathtub effect in this community was further aggravated by the immediate loss of a great number of experienced officers as a result of the numerous other drawdown programs implemented in addition to constraining accessions—i.e., VSI/SSB (Variable Separation Incentive/Special Separation Bonus), ADSC (Active Duty Service Commitment) waivers associated with the most liberal officer early-release program in history, TICS (Time in Commissioned Service) waivers, SERBs (Selective Early Retirement Boards), and RIFs. While these programs initially targeted year-groups populated above the ideal force-structure line (called TOPLINE), in the run up to the RIF of 1992, the desire to avoid or minimize RIF action was so intense that eligibility for VSI/SSB, ADSC waivers, etc., was increasingly liberalized, with a corresponding deemphasis on force-shaping priorities.

Further evidence of this deemphasis can be seen in the execution of the FY1992 RIF itself. Although force-shaping considerations largely drove the way in which year-groups were targeted for RIF action, the percentages of the year groups actually considered did not. Officers in the 1980–1984 year-groups had already had at least two opportunities to transfer their commissions into the regular Air Force[1]; those in the 1985 year-group had received only one such opportunity. Further, officers in the 1986–1989 year-groups had received *no* such opportunity, and most of these latter officers were ineligible for VSI/SSB or involuntary separation pay, owing to legal requirements for time in service to receive these monies.

Therefore, although RIFs were to be authorized from the reserve office groups only, leadership believed that officers having no chance, or just one chance, to move to a regular commission should be less

---

[1] In the early 1990s, only Air Force Academy graduates and distinguished ROTC graduates were given commissions in the regular Air Force when they went on active duty. The remainder had commissions in the reserves, even though they were on active duty. At certain points in their careers (attainment of a certain number of years of service or promotion), these reserve officers would be given the opportunity to convert their commissions to regular commissions. Some did not take this opportunity, and it was not uncommon to have majors or lieutenant colonels who had spent their adult life in the military with reserve commissions.

vulnerable to involuntary separation than those having received multiple opportunities. Additionally, it was decided by Air Force personnel managers that RIF-selection percentages for the 1986–1989 year-groups should be kept to an absolute minimum. These priorities are reflected in the final selection percentages, by year-group, for the FY1992 RIF: 1980–1984 = 95 percent; 1985 = 75 percent; 1986 = 25 percent; 1987 = 15 percent; and 1988–1989 = 6 percent.

This discussion is not meant to imply that the priorities of senior leadership for the drawdown were misguided. The senior leaders decided to emphasize one particular set of priorities, and these priorities could only be maintained at the expense of force-shaping priorities for the future. Because opportunities to hire back from the Reserve component are limited and because opportunities to hire mid-level personnel with military experience from the civilian community are extremely rare, the bathtub effect is nearly immune to solution until the affected year-groups retire. Coupling this effect with the wholesale release of junior- and mid-level officers in the non-rated career fields, we can readily see the origins of current manning imbalances across the spectrum of officer career fields.

Current senior analysts will say that they believe that analytic results about these consequences were not adequately presented or taken into account when the decisions were made.

Finally, in addition to being the origin of many of the manning imbalances the Air Force faces today in the non-rated officer community, the FY1992/1993 force drawdown also signaled the decline of strategic and operational force management in the personnel and functional communities. To implement and sustain strategic force management requires a substantial investment of time, analysis, and manpower. However, as manning levels plummeted throughout the Air Force and while deployment rates surged to four times that of the 1980s, many of the linkages evaporated between force management entities within the personnel community and between the personnel community and the functional communities. AFPC assignment teams no longer enjoyed the robust manning of the 1980s that allowed a concerted focus on force management issues, the AFPC Force Management Branch was dissolved, and career-field functional managers (where they continued to exist) often found their duties now to be considered part-time, or "additional duty" to their primary jobs.

The FY1992/1993 force drawdown can thus be seen as the seed of decline in strategic and operational force management. Yet, other changes during this timeframe contributed to accelerate the decline.

The Officer Volunteer Assignment System (OVAS)

During the FY1992/1993 force drawdown, the Air Force moved away from its long-standing, requirements-based officer assignment system, which emphasized the assignment of officers (involuntarily if necessary) to fill requirements and implemented the Officer Volunteer Assignment System (OVAS). OVAS sought to increase individual officers' visibility into positions coming available and to increase their voice and role in volunteering for and securing the jobs they desired. The underlying premise, or assumption, was that there would be a volunteer for every assignment that the Air Force needed to be filled.

A new Web-based system, the Assignment Management System (AMS), was developed and fielded so that job openings could be posted on an electronic bulletin board (EBB) and officers could volunteer for jobs, online, to the AFPC assignment teams.

While the visibility into requirements was widely seen as an improvement, there were downsides.

First, early on, *all* positions were posted on the EBB regardless of whether there was sufficient personnel inventory to fill them. Therefore, officers could volunteer for jobs that would not have been filled otherwise under the old system, which had explicitly set priorities for which positions would be filled first, based on policy, substantive knowledge, and, often, informal negotiations with the organizations having the open positions. However, under OVAS, failure to post all positions would generate criticism from officers in the career field who knew that jobs were coming open. Additionally, commanders and senior leaders were somewhat hamstrung in making internal realignments after position selection because there would be an accusation of "bait and switch" if someone volunteered for one job, was assigned there, and then was moved to another position considered more important to fill by local commanders.

Second, OVAS tended to cut commanders out of the assignment process because the previous process frequently consulted with them about the requirements for positions and the qualifications of people being considered. For the commanders whose people were moving to other positions, being cut out was especially frustrating because their role as front-line mentors was severely curtailed. Officers could volunteer whenever and wherever they chose, regardless of whether the commander—who now had no voice in the system—thought the timing or job was right. For the gaining commanders, who were initially cut out of the selection process as well, the situation was even more aggravating: They had little or no say in who showed up for the job because the candidates were only people who had volunteered. Their displeasure led quickly to the follow-on to OVAS, called "More Voice/More Choice," which gave the gaining commander the right to select from the list of volunteers; however, this selection process presented them with long lists of candidates (with little candidate information) for lower-level jobs in their organizations.

Eliminating the losing commanders' input disrupted the critical tactical-level role of mentors that commanders play in force management. Further, as OVAS, and then More Voice/More Choice, became a rules-based process focused only on decisions of the officer and the various individual commanders, the AFPC assignment teams' role as resource managers disappeared. In fact, they were no longer called "resource managers"; they were relabeled "assignment officers," reflecting the absence of responsibility for considering officer personnel development (OPD) in assignments and were forced into their new role as brokers of candidates.

As a result of this shift, the composition of the assignment teams at AFPC began to change. Senior and seasoned functional leaders were less critical to the assignment teams, and what was once "special duty" for them no longer seemed so "special." Consequently, over time, the strong bonds and linkages that had existed in the functional communities began to break down, and career field managers increasingly found themselves on their own, often with little knowledge of the personnel tools needed to appropriately manage their career fields. Taken together, these developments had a negative effect on operational-level and tactical-level force management.

Finally, the flaw that in the end spelled the demise of OVAS was that the initial premise of having a volunteer for every assignment turned out to be incorrect. The Air Force has many arduous, remote, hard-to-fill assignments that are nevertheless critical to mission accomplishment. As more and more of these types of assignments lay vacant for longer and longer periods of time, the frustration of commanders and senior leaders grew to the breaking point: the assignment system would have to be radically changed again.

The Air Force Assignment System

In 1998, the Air Force launched the new Air Force Assignment System (AFAS), which retained some positive features from the OVAS years, such as a Web-based system that allows officers visibility into upcoming openings. But it also returned to some of the values and tenets of the old Officer Assignment System.

First, AFAS fundamentally returned to a requirements-based system, although it seeks a balance among mission requirements, officer professional development, and individual desires. Losing commanders were brought back into the assignment process, making their input (mentorship) mandatory anytime an officer desires to submit preferences for his or her next assignment.

Further, assignment authority was returned to the assignment teams, and while gaining commanders may dispute an assignment match, they are no longer saddled with sifting through multiple lists of candidates to fill their requirements. AFPC assignment team members have been reestablished as "resource managers" and charged with the complex task of blending the mission requirements, OPD, commander input, and officer preference so critical to tactical force management. Most AFPC assignment teams are once again headed by experienced lieutenant colonels who partner with their Air Staff functional managers to help guide and sustain the health and welfare of their career fields.

While it therefore would appear that tactical force management is on the mend in the Air Force, the majority of those interviewed for this study recognize that there is still much to do, especially at the operational and strategic levels. Efforts are ongoing. Guidance for functional managers is being developed to help them better understand the full extent of their duties, as well as the tools and personnel entities at their disposal.

At the strategic level, however, there is much still to be done to establish linkages among the various entities involved in force management and to establish a governing entity with access and authority over the policy levers that shape the force. The time is ripe, as the Air Force seeks to implement the Chief of Staff of the Air Force's Force Development vision, through the Air Staff and out to the field, to establish these strategic linkages.

Bibliography

Ausink, John A., Jonathan A.K. Cave, Thomas Manacapilli, and Manuel J. Carillo, *User's Guide for the Compensation, Accessions, and Personnel Management (CAPM) Model*, Santa Monica, Calif.: RAND Corporation, MR-1688-AF/OSD, 2003.

Bigelow, James H., William W. Taylor, S. Craig Moore, and Brent Thomas, *Models of Operational Training in Fighter Squadrons*, Santa Monica, Calif.: RAND Corporation, MR-1701-AF, 2003.

Builder, Carl H., *The Icarus Syndrome: The Role of Air Power Theory in the Evolution and Fate of the U.S. Air Force*, New Brunswick, N.J.: Transaction Publications, 1994.

Dahlman, Carl J., Robert Kerchner, and David E. Thaler, *Setting Requirements for Maintenance Manpower in the U.S. Air Force*, Santa Monica, Calif.: RAND Corporation, MR-1436-AF, 2002.

Fernandez, Judith C., *A System for Allocating Selective Reenlistment Bonuses*, Santa Monica, Calif.: RAND Corporation, N-2829-FMP, 1989.

Gotz, Glenn A., and John J. McCall, *A Sequential Analysis of the Air Force Officer's Retirement Decision*, Santa Monica, Calif.: RAND Corporation, N-1013-AF, 1979.

Hafemeister, Rod, "Air Force Has People Surplus, but Trouble Matching Skills," *Air Force Times*, November 25, 2002.

Taylor, William W., James H. Bigelow, S. Craig Moore, Leslie Wickman, Brent Thomas, and Richard Marken, *Absorbing Air Force Fighter Pilots: Parameters, Problems, and Policy Options*, Santa Monica, Calif.: RAND Corporation, MR-1550-AF, 2002.

Thie, Harry J., Margaret C. Harrell, Jefferson P. Marquis, Kevin Brancato, Roland J. Yardley, Clifford M. Graf II, and Jerry Sollinger, *Aft and Fore: A Retrospective and Prospective Analysis of Navy Officer Management*, Santa Monica, Calif.: RAND Corporation, MR-1479-NAVY, 2003.

U.S. Air Force, *Career Development Guide for Scientists and Engineers*, published by SAF/AQR, 2003a. Available at http://www.safaq.hq.af.mil/aqre/mentoring/docs/3Jun_CDGt.pdf.

U.S. Air Force, *Chief's Sight Picture: Civilian Force Development*, May 2, 2003b. Available online at http://www.af.mil/lib/sight/Civilian_Force_Development.pdf.

U.S. Air Force, *Chief's Sight Picture: Enlisted Force Development*, April 28, 2003c. Available online at http://www.af.mil/lib/sight/Enlisted_Development.pdf.

U.S. Air Force, *Chief's Sight Picture: Officer Force Development—Spreading the Word*, October 7, 2003d. Available online at http://www.af.mil/viewpoint/OFD_Spreading_the_Word.pdf.

U.S. Air Force, *Classifying Military Personnel (Officer and Enlisted)*, Washington, D.C.: Air Force Instruction (AFI) 36-2101, April 30, 2001a.

U.S. Air Force, *Officer Classification*, Washington, D.C.: Air Force Instruction 36-2105, 2001b.

U.S. Air Force, *Personnel Strategic Plan: Fiscal Year 2004–2009*, Washington, D.C., 2004.

U.S. Air Force, *Total Force Development (Active Duty Officers)*, Washington, D.C.: Air Force Instruction 36-26, Vol. 1, September 1, 2003e.

U.S. Air Force, *The USAF Personnel Plan*, Vols. 1–8, USAFPP-1 through USAFPP-8, September 29, 1978.

U.S. Census Bureau, *Statistical Abstract of the United States 2003*, Washington, D.C., 2004, Table No. 517. Available online at http://www.census.gov/.

U.S. Department of Defense, *Defense Acquisition Management Policies and Procedures*, Washington, D.C.: Air Force Supplement 1 to DoDI 5000.2, 2003.

Walker, Warren E., and the Enlisted Force Management Project Team, *Design and Development of an Enlisted Force Management System for the Air Force*, Santa Monica, Calif.: RAND Corporation, R-3600-AF, 1991.

Vernez, Georges, S. Craig Moore, Steven Martino, and Jeffrey Yuan, "Improving the Development and Utilization of Air Force Space and Missile Officers," Santa Monica, Calif.: RAND Corporation, unpublished research.